MONITORIAL INSTRUCTIONS

FOR THE

USE OF SYMBOLIC LODGES

OF

FREE AND ACCEPTED MASONS

(1915)

William W. Perry
&
Jacob Dreher

ISBN 0-7661-0709-4

Request our FREE CATALOG of over 1,000
Rare Esoteric Books
Unavailable Elsewhere

Freemasonry * Akashic * Alchemy * Alternative Health * Ancient Civilizations * Anthroposophy * Astral * Astrology * Astronomy * Aura * Bacon, Francis * Bible Study * Blavatsky * Boehme * Cabalah * Cartomancy * Chakras * Clairvoyance * Comparative Religions * Divination * Druids * Eastern Thought * Egyptology * Esoterism * Essenes * Etheric * Extrasensory Perception * Gnosis * Gnosticism * Golden Dawn * Great White Brotherhood * Hermetics * Kabalah * Karma * Knights Templar * Kundalini * Magic * Meditation * Mediumship * Mesmerism * Metaphysics * Mithraism * Mystery Schools * Mysticism * Mythology * Numerology * Occultism * Palmistry * Pantheism * Paracelsus * Parapsychology * Philosophy * Plotinus * Prosperity & Success * Psychokinesis * Psychology * Pyramids * Qabalah * Reincarnation * Rosicrucian * Sacred Geometry * Secret Rituals * Secret Societies * Spiritism * Symbolism * Tarot * Telepathy * Theosophy * Transcendentalism * Upanishads * Vedanta * Wisdom * Yoga * *Plus Much More!*

KESSINGER PUBLISHING, LLC
http://www.kessingerpub.com
email: books@kessingerpub.com

EDITION 1915

Monitorial Instructions

For the Use of
Symbolic Lodges
...OF...
FREE AND ACCEPTED MASONS

Compiled and Arranged by
WILLIAM W. PERRY, Custodian of the Work
...and...
JACOB DREHER, Grand Lecturer
of the
MOST WORSHIPFUL GRAND LODGE
Free and Accepted Masons
OF WISCONSIN

Published by the
MASONIC SUPPLY COMPANY
Milwaukee, Wis.
1915

PRESS OF
S. E. TATE PRINTING COMPANY
MILWAUKEE, WIS.

PREFACE.

In presenting to the Craft the Monitorial Instructions, it is not the intention of the compilers to in any way supplant or set aside the valuable work done by Brother Melvin L. Youngs, for forty-five years Grand Lecturer of Wisconsin, in compiling his Masonic Guide.

We are willing to acknowledge his wisdom and experience in abridging the monitorial work, so as to place instruction within the reach of busy men.

This edition of Monitorial Instructions is a true copy of the one submitted to the M. W. Grand Lodge F. & A. M. of Wisconsin on Wednesday, June 10th, 1908, and *recommended* for use in Subordinate Lodges.

It is full and complete in every detail, and contains the exoteric Masonic Lectures in their entirety.

We trust this pocket edition of the work will be of service to the Craft.

Yours fraternally,
WILLIAM W. PERRY, Custodian,
and Grand Secretary.
JACOB DREHER, Grand Lecturer.

Amendment

In this edition a change is made on pages 103 and 157 in Installation Ceremonies. The last paragraph, "Finally, my brethren," etc., was amended to conform to ceremony for chartered lodges. The paragraph, as printed in former editions should have been used only in constituting new lodges.

MONITORIAL INSTRUCTIONS.

Visitors.

"In every clime a Mason may find a home, and in every land a brother."

The Lodge is his home, and every member present should give him a fraternal welcome, and make him feel that he is not a stranger but a brother among them.

Examinations.

Before admission the visitor must prove to the satisfaction of the Lodge that he is a Mason in good standing. The examination should be thorough, and sufficiently strict to prevent imposition.

Give the visiting brother a cordial welcome.

The examining committee is not expected to find out just how much the visiting brother knows of Masonry, but simply satisfy themselves, through the proper tests, that he is entitled to visit. More than this would seem unwarranted, and contrary to good Masonic ethics.

The following is a suitable form for a Test Oath to be administered:

I, ——, do hereby and hereon solemnly and sincerely swear that I have been regularly initiated, passed and raised to the sublime degree of Master Mason, in a regularly constituted Lodge of such; that I am not now under sentence of suspension or expulsion, and know of no just reason why I should not hold Masonic intercourse with my brethren. So help me God.

Mackey says the rigor and severity of the rules

and forms of a Masonic examination must never be weakened by undue partiality or unjustifiable delicacy.

Object of Masonry.

Harmony among the brethren is the first great object in Masonry. Not all those who have passed through our solemn ceremonies, and are called Masons, are truly such. Still, the general law holds good.

It is the duty of the Worshipful Master to preserve harmony among the members of his Lodge, and if a visiting brother is objected to by a member of the Lodge, the visitor must give precedence to the member who, by reason of his membership, has rights differing from those of the visitor.

The objection of a member should be heeded by the Worshipful Master, whether any reason be given therefor or not.

Balloting for Candidates.

In this, and many other Jurisdictions, one ballot only is required for the three degrees and for membership.

Great care should be taken before balloting to ascertain the worth and qualifications of the applicant. "Guard well the outer door," is a saying which cannot be too well heeded. But when accepted and initiated, he becomes a Mason; he then has rights differing from a profane.

Hence, objections to his advancement should only be made from the best of motives.

Communications.

The communications of a Lodge are either stated, special, or festival. By the Constitution of the Grand Lodge festival communications may be held on the days of Saint John the Baptist and Saint John the Evangelist, or for the installation of the officers of a Lodge.

Stated communications are those provided for by the By-Laws, to be held at regular times. The election of officers, the reception of all petitions for degrees or for membership and balloting upon same, must take place at stated communications, unless a special dispensation is granted by the Grand Master to do otherwise.

At all stated communications the Lodge must be opened in the Master Mason's degree, and in full form. In changing to a lower degree for the purpose of work, or for the examination of a candidate as to proficiency for advancement, it may be done in "short form," when a portion of the full opening is omitted; but never "without form or ceremony."

Special communications may be called by the Worshipful Master when, in his judgment, the interests of the Lodge require them, of which due and proper notice should be given to all members so far as practicable, or in open Lodge at a stated communication.

No business other than that for which it is called can be done at special communications.

Special communications called for work in the Entered Apprentice or Fellow Craft degrees should be opened and closed in the degree for which called.

Application for Degrees.

All applications for the degrees must be made in writing over the signature of the applicant, and in form prescribed by the Grand Lodge.

Blank Forms.

Secretaries of Lodges, when in need of petition blanks, both for the degrees and affiliation, and other stationery, should correspond with the Grand Secretary and obtain the proper forms used in this Grand Jurisdiction.

Care to be Exercised.

Great care should be taken, in filling out the petition, to ascertain whether the applicant has ever before applied to any Lodge for the degrees of Masonry, and if so, to what Lodge. In the event that petitioner has been rejected in another Lodge, careful investigation should be made to ascertain the nature of the objections, and the probable reasons why he did not then receive the degrees.

Proper Manner of Wearing Apron.

The habit of wearing the apron beneath the coat is not good Masonic form. On all public occasions the apron should be worn on the outside of the coat.

OPENING.

First, *Congregate.*—The Worshipful Master having signified his intention to proceed, every brother is expected to assume his necessary Masonic clothing, and if an officer, the jewel of his office, and repair to his appropriate station.

Second, *Purge.*—Ascertain, in an appropriate manner, the right of each one to be present.

Third, *Tile.*—Ascertain if the external avenues of the Lodge are securely guarded.

Fourth, *Lecture.*—When inquiry is made of the proper officers as to their knowledge of the Lectures and of the duties they will be called upon to perform, certain mystic rites are employed, by which each brother signifies his concurrence in the ceremonies and his knowledge of the degree in which the Lodge is opened.

OF BEHAVIOR IN THE LODGE WHILE IN SESSION.

You are not to hold private committees or separate conversation without leave from the Master, nor talk of anything impertinent, behave unseemly, nor interrupt the Master or Wardens or any brother speaking to the Master, nor behave yourselves ludicrously or jestingly while the Lodge is engaged in what is serious and solemn, nor use personal or unbecoming language upon any pretense whatever.

No private piques or quarrels must be brought within the door of the Lodge, far less any quarrels about religion, race or politics.

PRAYERS

That May be Used at the Opening of a Lodge.

Supreme Architect of the Universe, in Thy name we have assembled, and in Thy name we desire to proceed in all our doings. Grant that the sublime principles of Freemasonry may so subdue every discordant passion within us; so harmonize and enrich our hearts with Thine own love and goodness, that the Lodge at this time may humbly reflect that beauty and order which reign forever before Thy throne. Amen.

Response. So mote it be.

Or this:

Almighty God, grant us grace to so conduct the affairs of this Lodge that all we do, and all we think, and all we say, may be inspired by Thy wisdom, to the end that we may do Thy will, and to Thee shall be all honor and glory. Amen.

Response. So mote it be.

Or this:

May Heaven's blessing rest upon this, our meeting, thus happily begun; may it be conducted in order and closed in harmony. Amen.

Response. So mote it be.

CLOSING PRAYERS.

One of the Following May be Used:

Supreme Grand Master, Ruler of Heaven and Earth; Now that we are about to separate and return to our respective places of abode, wilt Thou be pleased so to influence our hearts and minds that we may each one of us practice out of the Lodge those great moral duties which are inculcated in it, and with reverence study and obey the laws which Thou hast given us in Thy holy Word. Amen.

Response. So mote it be.

Or this:

Supreme Architect of the Universe, accept our humble thanks for the many mercies and blessings which Thy bounty has conferred on us, and especially for this friendly and social intercourse. Pardon, we beseech Thee, whatever Thou hast seen amiss in us since we have been together; and continue to us Thy presence, protection and blessing. Make us sensible of the renewed obligations we are under to love Thee, and as we are about to separate, and return to our respective places of abode, wilt Thou be pleased so to influence our hearts and minds, that we may each one of us practice, out of the Lodge, those great moral duties which are inculcated in it, and with reverence study and obey the laws which Thou hast given us in Thy holy Word. Amen.

Response. So mote it be.

Any appropriate prayer may be used, in the discretion of the Worshipful Master.

CHARGE AT OPENING.

The ways of Virtue are beautiful. Knowledge is attained by degrees. Wisdom dwells with contemplation: there we must seek her. Let us then, brethren, apply ourselves with becoming zeal to the practice of the excellent principles inculcated by the Craft. Let us ever remember that the great objects of our fraternity are the restraint of improper desires and passions, the cultivation of an active benevolence, and the promotion of a correct knowledge of the duties we owe to God, our neighbor, and ourselves. Let us be united, and practice with assiduity the sacred tenets of the Craft. Let all private animosities, if any unhappily exist, give place to affection and brotherly love. It is a useless parade to talk of the subjection of irregular passions within the walls of the Lodge if we permit them to triumph in our intercourse with each other. Uniting in the grand design, let us be happy ourselves, and endeavor to promote the happiness of others. Let us cultivate the great moral virtues which are laid down on our Masonic Trestle-board and improve in everything that is good, amiable, and useful. Let the benign Genius of the Mystic Art preside over our councils, and under her sway let us act with a dignity becoming the high moral character of our venerable institution.

CHARGE AT CLOSING.

Brethren: You are now to quit this sacred retreat of friendship and virtue, to mix again with the world. Amidst its concerns and employments, forget not the duties you have heard so frequently inculcated and forcibly recommended in this Lodge. Be diligent, prudent, temperate, discreet. Remember that around this altar you have promised to befriend and relieve every brother who shall need your assistance. Remember that you have promised to remind him, in the most tender manner, of his failings, and aid in his reformation. Vindicate his character, when wrongfully traduced Suggest, in his behalf, the most candid and favorable circumstances. Is he justly reprehended? Let the world observe how Masons love one another.

These generous principles are to extend further. Every human being has a claim upon your kind offices. Do good unto all. Recommend it more especially to the household of the faithful.

By diligence in the duties of your respective callings; by liberal benevolence and diffusive charity; by constancy and fidelity in your friendships, discover the beneficial and happy effects of this ancient and honorable institution. Let it not be supposed that you have here labored in vain, and spent your strength for naught; for your work is with the Lord and your recompense with God.

Finally, brethren, be ye all of one mind; live in peace, and may the God of love and peace delight to dwell with and bless you.

BENEDICTION AT CLOSING.

May the blessing of Heaven rest upon us and all regular Masons. May brotherly love prevail, and every moral and social virtue unite and cement us. Amen.

Response. So mote it be.

ENTERED APPRENTICE.

FIRST SECTION.

During the preparation of a candidate only the Junior Deacon and Stewards should be in the preparation-room with him.

Levity and jesting with a candidate should not be indulged in.

Before the candidate is prepared for the First Degree, he should give unequivocal answers to the following questions, to be propounded by the Senior Deacon in the presence of the Secretary:

Do you seriously declare, upon your honor, that, unbiased by friends and uninfluenced by mercenary motives, you freely and voluntarily offer yourself a candidate for the mysteries of Freemasonry?

Do you seriously declare, upon your honor, that you are prompted to solicit the privileges of Masonry by a favorable opinion conceived of the institution, a desire for knowledge, and a sincere wish of being serviceable to your fellow creatures?

Do you seriously declare, upon your

honor, that you will cheerfully conform to all the ancient established usages and customs of the fraternity?

JUNIOR DEACON'S ADDRESS TO CANDIDATE.

Mr. ———, the institution of which you are about to become a member is one by no means of a light and trifling nature, but of high importance and deep solemnity. Masonry consists of a course of ancient hieroglyphical and moral instructions, taught according to ancient usage, by types, emblems and allegorical figures. Even the ceremony of your gaining admission within these walls is emblematic of an event which all must sooner or later experience. It is emblematic of *   *   *   *   *
 *   *   *   *   *   *

You are doubtless aware that whatever a man may possess here on earth, whether it be titles, honors, or even his own reputation, will not gain him admission into the Celestial Lodge above; but, previous to his gaining admission there, he must become poor and penniless, * * *

dependent on the sovereign will of our Supreme Grand Master; and, in order to impress these truths more forcibly upon your mind, it is necessary that you * *
* * * * * *
Are you willing to submit to these regulations? (I am.) We will prepare you in a suitable manner for your initiation, as all have been prepared who have gone this way before you.

PRAYERS

That May be Used at the Reception of a Candidate.

Vouchsafe Thine aid, Almighty Father of the Universe, to this, our present convention. Grant that this candidate for Masonry may dedicate and devote his life to Thy service, and become a true and faithful brother among us. Endue him with a competency of Thy Divine wisdom, that by the secrets of our art he may be better enabled to display the beauties of Brotherly Love, Relief and Truth, to the honor and glory of Thy Holy Name. Amen.

Response. So mote it be.

Or this:

Almighty God, in whom alone is our trust, and whose watchful care is ever over us, bless us in the exercise of those kind and social affections Thou hast given us. May we cherish and display them as our honor and our joy. May this, our friend, who is now to become our brother, devote his life to Thy service, and rightfully consider the principles of his engagements. May he be endowed with wisdom to direct him in all his ways; strength to support him in all his difficulties, and beauty to adorn his moral conduct. Let Thy Fatherly hand ever be over him, and so lead him in the knowledge and the obedience of Thy Divine Laws that, having finished his course below, he may at last pass peacefully and joyfully to those mansions prepared for him in Thy Temple above —that house not made with hands, eternal in the heavens. Amen.

Response. So mote it be.

Any other suitable prayer may be used.

LESSON
To be Read at Every Initiation.

Behold, how good and how pleasant it is for brethren to dwell together in unity!

It is like the precious ointment upon the head, that ran down upon the beard, even Aaron's beard, that went down to the skirts of his garments.

As the dew of Hermon, and as the dew that descended upon the mountains of Zion; for there the Lord commanded the blessing, even life for evermore.—Psalm cxxxiii.

The following hymn may be used in place of the Lesson:

TUNE—Auld Lang Syne.

Behold! how pleasant and how good,
　For brethren such as we,
Of the Accepted Brotherhood,
　To dwell in unity.

'Tis like the oil on Aaron's head,
　Which to his feet distils;
Like Hermon's dew, so richly shed,
　On Zion's sacred hills.

For there the Lord of Light and Love,
　A blessing sent with power:
O, may we all this blessing prove,
　E'en life for evermore.

18   MONITORIAL INSTRUCTIONS.

On Friendship's altar rising here,
Our hands now plighted be,
To live in love with hearts sincere,
In peace and unity.

CIRCUMAMBULATION.

* * * * * *

It is a duty incumbent on every Master of a Lodge, before the full ceremony of initiation takes place, to explain to the candidate the nature of his solemn engagements, and, in a manner peculiar to Masons alone, to require his cheerful acquiescence.

* * * * * *

In the beginning God created the heaven and the earth.

And the earth was without form, and void, and darkness was upon the face of the deep. And the Spirit of God moved upon the face of the waters.

And God said, Let there be light: and there was light.

* * * * * *

The Holy Bible is to rule and guide our faith; the Square, to square our actions; and the Compasses, to circumscribe and keep us within due bounds with all mankind * * * * *

* * * * * *

As the sun rules the day and the moon governs the night, so ought the Worshipful Master to endeavor to rule and govern his Lodge with equal regularity.
* * * * * *
* * * with a lamb-skin, or white leather apron. It is an emblem of innocence and the badge of a Mason; more ancient than the Golden Fleece or Roman Eagle; more honorable than the Star and Garter, or any other order that could be conferred upon you at this time, or any future period, by king, prince, potentate, or any other person, except he be a Mason. It is hoped that you will wear it with equal pleasure to yourself and honor to the fraternity. * * * *
* * * * * *
* * * * Let this make a deep and lasting impression upon your mind. * * *

You now stand   * * * *   a just and upright Mason * * *

WORKING TOOLS.

* * * The working tools of an Entered Apprentice, which are the

Twenty-four inch Gauge and the Common Gavel.

The Twenty-four inch Gauge is an instrument made use of by operative masons, to measure and lay out their work; but we, as Free and Accepted Masons, are taught to make use of it for the more noble and glorious purpose of dividing our time. It being divided into twenty-four equal parts, is emblematic of the twenty-four hours of the day, which we are taught to divide into three equal parts, whereby we find eight hours for the service of God and the relief of a distressed worthy brother, eight for our usual vocations, and eight for refreshment and sleep.

The Common Gavel is an instrument made use of by operative masons, to break off the corners of rough stones, the better to fit them for the builder's use; but we, as Free and Accepted Masons, are taught to make use of it for the more noble and glorious purpose of divesting our minds and consciences of the vices and superfluities of life, thereby fitting us as living stones for that spiritual building, that house not made with hands, eternal in the heavens.

*   *   *   *   *   *

SECOND SECTION.

The following Lessons and Scripture quotations are appropriately introduced:

At the building of King Solomon's Temple there was not heard the sound of ax, hammer, or any tool of iron. * * * *

It is the internal and not the external qualifications of a man that should recommend him to be made a Mason.

We read in the Book of Ruth that it was the manner in former time concerning redeeming and changing, that to confirm all things a man plucked off his shoe and gave it to his neighbor: this was testimony in Israel. * * * *

Ask and ye shall receive; seek and ye shall find; knock and it shall be opened unto you.

No man should ever engage in any great or important undertaking without first invoking the blessing of Deity.

No Atheist can be made a Mason.

The left is said to be the weaker part of man.

The right hand was said by our ancient brethren to be the seat of fidelity, which we sometimes see represented by two right hands joined; at others, by two human figures holding each other by the right hand. * * * *

The lamb has, in all ages, been deemed an emblem of innocence; he, therefore, who wears the lambskin as the badge of a Mason, is thereby continually reminded of that purity of life and conduct which is so essentially necessary to his gaining admission into the Celestial Lodge above, where the Supreme Architect of the Universe presides.

.* * * * * *.

Should you ever meet a friend * * * * * * * destitute circumstances, you should contribute as liberally to his relief as you could without material injury to yourself.

In operative Masonry, the first stone of a building is usually laid in the northeast corner. * * * *

THIRD SECTION.

The Third Section of this degree relates more particularly to the Lodge. It explains its form, supports, covering, furniture, ornaments, lights and jewels, how situated and to whom dedicated.

A LODGE.

A Lodge is composed of a constitutional number of Masons, duly assembled, with the Holy Bible, Square and Compasses, and a charter or warrant empowering them to work.

Our ancient brethren were accustomed to meet on a high hill or in a low vale. * * * *

FORM OF A LODGE.

The form of a Lodge is an oblong square, extending from east to west and between the north and south, from the center to the surface, and from the earth to the highest Heaven. It is said to be thus extensive to denote the universality of Masonry, and that Masonic charity should be equally extensive.

SUPPORTS.

It is metaphorically supported by three great pillars, denominated Wisdom, Strength and Beauty, because it is necessary that there should be wisdom to contrive, strength to support, and beauty to adorn all great and important undertakings.

These pillars are represented by the three principal officers of the Lodge, the W. M., S. and J. Wardens.

The W. M. represents the pillar of wisdom. * * *

The S. W. represents the pillar of strength. * * *

The J. W. represents the pillar of beauty. * * *

COVERING.

The covering of a Lodge is the clouded canopy, or starry - decked

Heaven, where all good Masons hope at last to arrive, by the aid of that mysterious ladder which Jacob, in his vision, saw extending from earth to Heaven, the three principal rounds of which are denominated Faith, Hope and Charity, and admonish us to have faith in God, hope in immortality, and charity to all mankind.

The greatest of these is Charity; for our Faith will be lost in sight, Hope ends in fruition, but Charity extends beyond the grave, through the boundless realms of eternity.

FURNITURE.

The furniture of a Lodge is the Holy Bible, Square and Compasses. The Bible is dedicated to God, the Square to the Master, and the Compasses to the Craft.

The Bible is dedicated to God, because it is the inestimable gift of God to man, * * *; the Square to the Master, because it is the proper emblem of his office, and should continually remind him of the duty he owes to the Lodge over which he is elected to preside; and the Compasses to the Craft, for by a due attention to their use they are taught to circumscribe their desires and keep their passions within due bounds with all mankind.

ORNAMENTS.

The ornaments of a Lodge are the Mosaic Pavement, the Indented Tessel, and the Blazing Star.

The Mosaic Pavement is a representation of the ground floor of King Solomon's Temple; the Indented Tessel, of that beautiful tesselated border or skirting which surrounded it.

The Mosaic Pavement is emblematic of human life, checkered with good and evil; the Beautiful Border which surrounds it, of those blessings and comforts which surround us, and which we hope to obtain by a faithful reliance on Divine Providence, which is hieroglyphically represented by the Blazing Star in the center.

LIGHTS.

A Lodge has three lights, situated east, west and south—none in the north.

* * * *

JEWELS.

A Lodge has six jewels—three immovable and three movable.

The immovable Jewels* are the Square, Level and Plumb. The Square teaches morality, the Level equality, and the Plumb rectitude of conduct.

The movable Jewels are the Rough Ashlar, the Perfect Ashlar, and the Trestle-board.

The Rough Ashlar is a stone taken from the quarry in its rude and natural state. The Perfect Ashlar is a stone made ready by the hands of the workman, to be adjusted by the working tools of the Fellow Craft. The Trestle-board is for the master workman to draw his designs upon.

By the Rough Ashlar we are reminded of our rude and imperfect state by nature; by the Perfect Ashlar, of that state of perfection at which we hope to arrive by a virtuous education, our own en-

---

*The Square, Level and Plumb are called immovable, because worn by the Worshipful Master, Senior and Junior Wardens, and they are always to be found in the East, West and South.

deavors, and the blessing of God; and by the Trestle-board we are also reminded that, as the operative workman erects his temporal building agreeably to the rules and designs laid down by the master on his Trestle-board, so should we, both operative and speculative, endeavor to erect our spiritual building agreeably to the rules and designs laid down by the Supreme Architect of the Universe in the Great Book of Nature and Revelation, which is our spiritual, moral and Masonic Trestle-board.

LODGES—HOW SITUATED.

All Lodges are, or ought to be, situated due east and west, because King Solomon's Temple was so situated. King Solomon's Temple was so situated because, after Moses had safely conducted the Children of Israel through the Red Sea, when pursued by Pharaoh and his hosts, he, by Divine command, erected a tabernacle and situated it due east and west, to perpetuate the remembrance of that remarkable east wind which wrought their mighty deliverance, and likewise the better to receive the rays of the rising sun. As this tabernacle was a model for King Solomon's Temple, so ought all Lodges to be situated due east and west.

TO WHOM DEDICATED.

Lodges were anciently dedicated to King Solomon, who is said to have been our first Most Excellent Grand Master. But Masons, in modern times, dedicate theirs to St. John the Baptist and St. John the Evangelist, who were two eminent Christian patrons of Masonry; and since their time there is, or ought to be, represented in every regular and well-governed Lodge, a certain Point within a Circle; the Point representing an individual brother, the Circle the boundary line of his duty, beyond which he is never to suffer his passions or prejudices to betray him. This circle is embordered by two perpendicular parallel lines, representing St. John the Baptist and St. John the Evangelist; upon the top rests the Holy Scriptures. In passing around this Circle we necessarily touch upon both lines, as well as upon the Holy Scriptures, and while a Mason keeps himself thus circumscribed, it is impossible that he should materially err.

TENETS.

The tenets of our profession are Brotherly Love, Relief and Truth.

Brotherly Love.

By the exercise of brotherly love we are taught to regard the whole human species as one family—the high and low, the rich and poor; who, as created by one Almighty Parent, and inhabitants of the same planet, are to aid, support, and protect each other. On this principle Masonry unites men of every country, sect and opinion, and conciliates true friendship among those who might otherwise have remained at a perpetual distance.

Relief.

To relieve the distressed is a duty incumbent on all men, but particularly on Masons, who are linked together by an indissoluble chain of sincere affection.

To soothe the unhappy, to sympathize with their misfortunes, to compassionate their miseries, and to restore peace to their troubled minds, is the grand aim we have in view. On this basis we form our friendships and establish our connections.

Truth.

Truth is a Divine attribute, and the foundation of every virtue. To be good and true is the first lesson we are taught in Masonry. On this theme we contemplate, and by its dictates endeavor to regulate our conduct. Hence, while influenced by this principle, hypocrisy and deceit are unknown among us, sincerity and plain dealing distinguish us, and the heart and tongue join in promoting each other's welfare and rejoicing in each other's prosperity.

* * * * * *

They allude to the four cardinal virtues, Temperance, Fortitude, Prudence and Justice.

TEMPERANCE.

Temperance is that due restraint upon

our affections and passions which renders the body tame and governable, and frees the mind from the allurements of vice. This virtue should be the constant practice of every Mason, as he is thereby taught to avoid excess, or contracting any licentious or vicious habit, the indulgence of which might lead him to disclose some of those valuable secrets which he has promised to conceal and never reveal, and which would consequently subject him to the contempt and detestation of all good Masons, * * *

FORTITUDE.

Fortitude is that noble and steady purpose of the mind whereby we are enabled to undergo any pain, peril or danger when prudentially deemed expedient. This virtue is equally distant from rashness and cowardice, and, like the former, should be deeply impressed upon the mind of every Mason, as a safeguard or security against any illegal attack that may be made, by force or otherwise, to extort from him any of those valuable secrets with which he has been so solemnly intrusted, and which was emblematically represented upon his first admission into the Lodge,   *   *   *

PRUDENCE.

Prudence teaches us to regulate our lives and actions agreeably to the dictates of reason, and is that habit by which we wisely judge, and prudentially determine, on all things relative to our present as well as to our future happiness. This virtue should be the peculiar characteristic of every Mason, not only for the government of his conduct while in the Lodge, but also when abroad in the world. It should be particularly attended to in all strange and mixed companies, never to let fall the least sign, token or word whereby the secrets of Masonry might be unlawfully obtained, *   *   *   *

JUSTICE.

Justice is that standard or boundary of right which enables us to render to every man his just due, without distinction. This virtue is not only consistent with Divine and human laws, but is the very cement and support of civil society; and as justice in a great measure constitutes the really good man, so should it be the invariable practice of every Mason never to deviate from the minutest principles thereof, * * * * * * * * Entered Apprentices served their Masters with

FREEDOM, FERVENCY AND ZEAL,

which are emblematically represented by Chalk, Charcoal, and Clay.

There is nothing freer than Chalk, the slightest touch of which leaves a trace behind.

There is nothing more fervent than Charcoal, to which, when well ignited, the most obdurate metals will yield.

Nothing more zealous than Clay, or our Mother Earth, which is continually imparting for man's necessities, and as constantly reminding us that as from it we came so to it we must all sooner or later return.

The following may be used:

Our Mother Earth alone, of all the elements, has never proved unfriendly to man; the bodies of water deluge him with rain, oppress him with hail, and drown him with inundations. The air rushes in storms, prepares the tempest, and lights up the volcano; but the earth, ever kind and indulgent, is found subservient to his wishes. Though constantly harassed, more to furnish the luxuries than the necessaries of life, she never refuses her accustomed yield, spreading his path with flowers and his table with plenty; though she produces poison, still she supplies the antidote, and returns with interest every good committed to her care; and when at last he is called upon to pass through the "dark valley of the shadow of Death," she once more receives him and piously covers his remains within her bosom. This admonishes us that from it we came and to it we must shortly return.

Such is the arrangement of the different sections of the First Lecture, which, with the forms adopted for the opening and closing of a Lodge, comprehends the whole of the first degree of Masonry.

The whole is a regular system of morality veiled in allegory, which will unfold its beauties to the candid and industrious inquirer.

CHARGE AT INITIATION.

Brother: As you are now introduced into the first principles of Masonry, I congratulate you on being accepted into this Ancient and Honorable Fraternity—ancient, as having subsisted from time immemorial; and honorable, as tending, in every particular, so to render all men who will be conformable to its precepts. No institution was ever raised on a better principle or more solid foundation, nor were ever more excellent rules and useful maxims laid down than are inculcated in the several Masonic lectures. The greatest and best of men in all ages have been encouragers and promoters of the art, and have never deemed it derogatory to their dignity to level themselves with the fraternity, extend their privileges, and patronize their assemblies.

There are three great duties which, as a Mason, you are charged to inculcate —to God, your neighbor, and yourself. To God, in never mentioning His name but with that reverential awe which is due from a creature to his Creator; to implore His aid in all your laudable undertakings, and to esteem Him as the chief good. To your neighbor, in acting upon the square, and doing unto him as you wish he should do unto you. And to yourself, in avoiding all irregularity and intemperance, which may impair your faculties or debase the dignity of your profession. A zealous attachment to these duties will insure public and private esteem.

In the State you are to be a quiet and peaceful subject, true to your government and just to your country. You are not to countenance disloyalty or rebellion, but patiently submit to legal authority, and conform with cheerfulness to the government of the country in which you live.

In your outward demeanor be particularly careful to avoid censure or reproach. Let not interest, favor or prejudice bias your integrity, or influence you to be guilty of a dishonorable action.

Although your frequent appearance at our regular meetings is earnestly solicited, yet it is not meant that Masonry should interfere with your necessary vocations, for these are on no account to be neglected. Neither are you to suffer your zeal for the institution to lead you into argument with those who, through ignorance, may ridicule it.

At your leisure hours, that you may improve in Masonic knowledge, you are to converse with well-informed brethren, who will be always as ready to give as you will be ready to receive instruction.

Finally, keep sacred and inviolable the mysteries of the fraternity, as these are to distinguish you from the rest of the community, and mark your consequence among Masons.

If, in the circle of your acquaintance, you find a person desirous of being initiated into Masonry, be particularly careful not to recommend him unless you are convinced he will conform to our rules, that the honor, glory, and reputation of the institution may be firmly established, and the world at large convinced of its good effects.

* * * * * *

FELLOW CRAFT.

FIRST SECTION.

* * * * * *

The Square of Virtue should be the rule and guide of our conduct in all future transactions with mankind.

* * * * * *

SCRIPTURE LESSON TO BE READ.

Thus he shewed me; and behold, the Lord stood upon a wall made by a plumb-line, with a plumb-line in His hand.

And the Lord said unto me: Amos, what seest thou? And I said: A plumb-line. Then said the Lord: Behold, I will set a plumb-line in the midst of my people Israel; I will not again pass by them any more.—Amos vii, 7, 8.

* * * * * *

The following hymn may be used instead of the Lesson:

TUNE—What Fairy-Like Music.

Come Craftsmen, assembled, our pleasure to share
Who work by the Plumb and remember the Square;

While trav'ling in love on the Level of time,
Sweet hope shall light on to a far better clime.

We'll seek in our labors the Spirit Divine,
Our temple to bless, and our hearts to refine;
And thus to our altar a tribute we'll bring,
While, joined in true friendship, our anthem we sing.

See Order and Beauty rise gently to view,
Each Brother a column, so perfect and true.
When Order shall cease, and when temples decay,
May each fairer columns immortal survey.

* * * * * *

In the beginning God created the heaven and the earth.

And the earth was without form, and void; and darkness was upon the face of the deep. And the Spirit of God moved upon the face of the waters.

And God said, Let there be light: and there was light.

* * * * * *

THE WORKING TOOLS.

The working tools of a Fellow Craft are the Plumb, Square and Level.

The Plumb is an instrument made use of by operative masons to raise perpendiculars; the Square, to square their work; and the Level to prove horizontals; but we, as Free and Accepted Masons, are taught to make use of them for more noble and glorious purposes. The Plumb admonishes us to walk uprightly in our several stations before God and man, squaring our actions by the Square of Virtue, and ever remembering that we are traveling upon the Level of time to that "undiscovered country from whose bourne no traveler returns."

* * * * * *

SECOND SECTION.

Masonry is considered under two denominations—Operative and Speculative.

By Operative Masonry we allude to a proper application of the useful rules of architecture, whence a structure will derive figure, strength and beauty, and whence will result a due proportion and a just correspondence in all its parts. It furnishes us with dwellings and convenient shelter from the vicissitudes and inclemencies of seasons; and while it displays the effects of human wisdom, as well in the choice as in the arrangement of the sundry materials of which an edifice is composed, it demonstrates that a fund of science and industry is implanted in man for the best, most salutary and beneficent purposes.

By Speculative Masonry we learn to subdue the passions, act upon the square, keep a tongue of good report, maintain secrecy, and practice charity. It is so far interwoven with religion as to lay us under obligations to pay that rational homage to the Deity, which at once constitutes our duty and our happiness. It leads the contemplative to view with reverence and admiration the glorious works of creation, and inspires him with the most exalted ideas of the perfections of his Divine Creator.

We work in Speculative Masonry only, but our ancient brethren wrought in both Operative and Speculative. They worked at the building of King Solomon's Temple and many other sacred and Masonic edifices.

They worked six days before receiving

their wages, but did not work on the seventh, for in six days God created the Heaven and the earth, and rested upon the seventh day; the seventh, therefore, our ancient brethren consecrated as a day of rest from their labors, thereby enjoying frequent opportunities to contemplate the glorious works of creation, and to adore their great Creator.

* * * * * *

PILLARS.

* * * * * *

Peace, Unity and Plenty.

* * * * * *

These globes are two artificial spherical bodies, on the convex surfaces of which are represented the countries, seas, and various parts of the earth, the face of the heavens, the planetary revolutions, and other important particulars.

The sphere with the parts of the earth delineated on its surface is called the terrestrial globe, and that with the constellations and other heavenly bodies, the celestial globe.

THE USE OF THE GLOBES.

Their principal use, besides serving as maps to distinguish the outward parts of the earth and the situation of the fixed stars, is to illustrate and explain the phenomena arising from the annual revolution of the earth around the sun, and the diurnal rotation upon its own axis.

They are invaluable instruments for improving the mind, and giving it the most distinct idea of any problem or proposition, as well as enabling it to solve the same. Contemplating these bodies, we are inspired with a due reverence for the Deity and His works, and are induced to encourage the studies of Astronomy, Geography, Navigation, and the arts dependent on them, by which society has been so much benefited.

* * * * * *

3—5—7

There are three degrees conferred in every Lodge. The three principal officers of a Lodge are the Worshipful Master, Senior and Junior Wardens.

* * * * * *

ORDER IN ARCHITECTURE.

By order in architecture is meant a system of all the members, proportions and ornaments of columns and pilasters; or, it is a regular arrangement of the projecting parts of a building which united with those of a column form a beautiful, perfect and complete whole.

OF ITS ANTIQUITY.

From the first formation of society order in architecture may be traced. When the rigor of seasons obliged men to contrive shelter from the inclemency of the weather, we learn that they first planted trees on end, and then laid others across the top to support a covering. The bands which connected those trees at top and bottom are said to have given rise to the idea of the base and capital of pillars; and from this simple hint originally proceeded the more improved art of architecture.

CLASSIFICATION.

The five orders are thus classed: The Tuscan, Doric, Ionic, Corinthian, and Composite.

FELLOW CRAFT.

THE TUSCAN

Is the most simple and solid of the five orders. It was invented in Tuscany, whence it derives its name. Its column is seven diameters high; and its capital, base, and entablature have but few moldings. The simplicity of the construction of this column renders it eligible where ornament would be superfluous.

THE DORIC,

Which is plain and natural, is the most ancient, and was invented by the Greeks. Its column is eight diameters high, and has seldom any ornaments on base or capital, except moldings, though the frieze is distinguished by triglyphs and metopes, and triglyphs compose the ornaments of the frieze.

The Doric is the best proportioned of all the orders. The several parts of which it is composed are founded on the natural position of solid bodies. In its first invention it was more simple than in its present state. In after times, when it began to be adorned, it gained the name of Doric; for when it was constructed in its primitive and simple form, the name of Tuscan was conferred on it. Hence the Tuscan precedes the Doric in rank, on account of its resemblance to that pillar in its original state.

THE IONIC

Bears a kind of mean proportion between the more solid and delicate orders. Its column is nine diameters high, its capital is adorned with volutes, and its cornice has dentils. There is both delicacy and ingenuity displayed in this pillar, the invention of which is attributed to the Ionians, as the famous temple of Diana at Ephesus was of this order. It is said to have been formed after the model of an agreeable young woman, as a contrast to the Doric order, which was formed after that of a strong, robust man.

THE CORINTHIAN,

The richest of the five orders, is deemed a masterpiece of art. Its column is ten diameters high, and its capital is adorned with two rows of leaves and eight volutes, which sustain the abacus. The frieze is ornamented with curious devices, the cornice with dentils and modillions. This order is used in stately and superb structures.

It was invented at Corinth, by Callimachus, who is said to have taken the hint of the capital of this pillar from the following remarkable circumstance: Accidentally passing by the tomb of a young lady, he perceived a basket of toys covered with tile, placed over an acanthus root, having been left there by her nurse. As the branches grew up, they encompassed the basket, till, arriving at the tile, they met with an obstruction, and bent downward. Callimachus, struck with the object, set about imitating the figure; the vase of the capital he made to represent the basket; the abacus, the tile; and the volutes, the bending leaves.

THE COMPOSITE

Is compounded of the other orders, and was contrived by the Romans. Its capital has the two rows of leaves of the Corinthian, and the volutes of the Ionic. Its column has quarter-rounds, as the Tuscan and Doric orders, is ten diameters high, and its cornice has dentils, or simple modillions. This pillar is generally found in buildings where strength, elegance and beauty are displayed.

OF THE INVENTION OF ORDER IN ARCHITECTURE.

The ancient and original Orders of Architecture revered by Masons, are no more than three—the Ionic, Doric and Corinthian, which were invented by the Greeks. To these the Romans have added two: the Tuscan, which they made plainer than the Doric, and the Composite, which was more ornamental, if not more beautiful, than the Corinthian. The first three orders alone, however, show invention and particular character, and essentially differ from each other; the two others have nothing but what is borrowed, and differ only accidentally; the Tuscan is the Doric in its earliest state; and the Composite is the Corinthian enriched with the Ionic. To the Greeks, therefore, and not to the Romans, are we indebted for what is great, judicious, and distinct in architecture.

ANCIENT ORDERS.

Of these five orders, the Ionic, Doric, and Corinthian, as the most ancient, are most esteemed by Masons. The Ionic, from the skill and ingenuity displayed in its construction, is emblematic of the column of Wisdom, which is situated in the east part of the Lodge, and is represented by the Worshipful Master; the Doric, from the massive strength of its structure, is emblematic of the column of Strength, which is situated in the west part of the Lodge, and is represented by the Senior Warden; and the Corinthian, from the exuberance of its ornaments, is emblematic of the column of Beauty, which is situated in the south part of the Lodge, and is represented by the Junior Warden.

* * * * * *

THE FIVE HUMAN SENSES,

Which are Hearing, Seeing, Feeling, Smelling, and Tasting.

HEARING

Is that sense by which we distinguish sounds, and are capable of enjoying all the agreeable charms of music. By it we are enabled to enjoy the pleasures of society, and reciprocally to communicate to each other our thoughts and intentions, our purposes and desires, and thus our reason is capable of exerting its utmost power and energy.

The wise and beneficent Author of Nature intended, by the formation of this sense, that we should be social creatures, and receive the greatest and most important part of our knowledge by the information of others. For these purposes, we are endowed with hearing, that by a proper exertion of our rational powers, our happiness may be complete.

SEEING

Is that sense by which we distinguish objects, and in an instant of time, without change of place or situation, view armies in battle array, figures of the most stately structures, and all the agreeable variety displayed in the landscape of Nature.

By this sense, we find our way on the pathless ocean, traverse the globe of earth, determine its figure and dimensions, and delineate any region or quarter of it. By it we measure the planetary orbs, and make new discoveries in the sphere of the fixed stars. Nay, more; by it we perceive the tempers and dispositions, the passions and affections, of our fellow-creatures, when they wish most to conceal them; so that, though the tongue may be taught to lie and dissemble, the countenance would display the hypocrisy to the discerning eye. In fine, the rays of light which administer to this sense are the most astonishing part of the animated creation, and render the eye a peculiar object of admiration.

Of all the faculties, sight is the noblest. The structure of the eye and its appurtenances evince the admirable contrivance of Nature for performing all its various external and internal motions, while the variety displayed in the eyes of different animals, suited to their several ways of life, clearly demonstrate this organ to be the masterpiece of Nature's work.

FEELING

Is that sense by which we distinguish the different qualities of bodies, such as heat and cold, hardness and softness, roughness and smoothness, figure, solidity, motion, and extension.

SMELLING

Is that sense by which we distinguish odors, the various kinds of which convey different impressions to the mind. Animal and vegetable bodies, and, indeed, most other bodies, while exposed to the air, continually send forth effluvia of vast subtility, as well in the state of life and growth as in the state of fermentation and putrefaction. These effluvia being drawn into the nostrils along with the air, are the means by which all bodies are smelled. Hence it is evident that there is a manifest appearance of design in the great Creator's having planted the organ of smell in the inside of that canal through which the air continually passes in respiration.

TASTING

Enables us to make a proper distinction in the choice of our food. The organ of this sense guards the entrance of the alimentary canal, as that of smelling guards the entrance of the canal for respiration. From the situation of both these organs, it is plain that they were intended by Nature to distinguish wholesome food from that which is nauseous. Everything that enters into the stomach must undergo the scrutiny of tasting; and by it we are capable of discerning the changes which the same body undergoes in the different compositions of art, cookery, chemistry, pharmacy, etc.

Smelling and tasting are inseparably connected; and it is by the unnatural kind of life men commonly lead in society, that these senses are rendered less fit to perform their natural offices.

The first three, Hearing, Seeing and Feeling, * * * * *

* * * * * *

THE SEVEN LIBERAL ARTS AND SCIENCES,

Which are Grammar, Rhetoric, Logic, Arithmetic, Geometry, Music and Astronomy.

GRAMMAR

Is the key by which alone the door can be opened to the understanding of speech. It is Grammar which reveals the admirable art of language, and unfolds its various constituent parts—its names, definitions, and respective offices; it unravels, as it were, the thread of which the web of speech is composed. These reflections seldom occur to any one before their acquaintance with the art; yet it is most certain that, without a knowledge of Grammar, it is very difficult to speak with propriety, precision, and purity.

RHETORIC.

It is by Rhetoric that the art of speaking eloquently is acquired. To be an eloquent speaker, in the proper sense of the word, is far from being either a common or an easy attainment; it is the art of being persuasive and commanding;

the art, not only of pleasing the fancy, but of speaking both to the understanding and to the heart.

LOGIC

Is that science which directs us how to form clear and distinct ideas of things, and thereby prevents us from being misled by their similitude or resemblance. Of all the human sciences, that concerning man is certainly most worthy of the human mind, and the proper manner of conducting its several powers in the attainment of truth and knowledge. This science ought to be cultivated as the foundation or groundwork of our inquiries; particularly in the pursuit of those sublime principles which claim our attention as Masons.

ARITHMETIC

Is the art of numbering, or that part of the mathematics which considers the properties of numbers in general. We have but a very imperfect idea of things without quantity, and as imperfect of quantity itself, without the help of Arithmetic. All the works of the Almighty are made in number, weight, and measure; therefore, to understand them rightly, we ought to understand arithmetical calculations; and the greater advancement we make in the mathematical sciences, the more capable we shall be of considering such things as are the ordinary objects of our conceptions, and be thereby led to a more comprehensive knowledge of our great Creator and the works of the creation.

GEOMETRY

Treats of the powers and properties of magnitudes in general, where length, breadth and thickness are considered—from a point to a line, from a line to a superficies, and from a superficies to a solid.

A point is the beginning of all geometrical matter.

A line is a continuation of the same.

A superficies is length and breadth, without a given thickness.

A solid is length and breadth, with a given thickness, which forms a cube, and comprehends the whole.

MUSIC

Is that elevated science which affects the passions by sound. There are few who have not felt its charms, and acknowledged its expression to be intelligible to the heart. It is a language of delightful sensations, far more eloquent than words; it breathes to the ear the clearest intimations; it touches and gently agitates the agreeable and sublime passions; it wraps us in melancholy, and elevates us in joy; it dissolves and inflames; it melts us in tenderness, and excites us to war. This science is truly congenial to the nature of man, for by its powerful charms the most discordant passions may be harmonized, and brought into perfect unison; but it never sounds with such seraphic harmony as when employed in singing hymns of gratitude to the Creator of the universe.

ASTRONOMY

Is that sublime science which inspires the contemplative mind to soar aloft, and read the wisdom, strength and beauty of the great Creator in the heavens. How nobly eloquent of the Deity is the celestial hemisphere!—spangled with the most magnificent heralds of His infinite glory! They speak to the whole universe; for there is no speech so barbarous but their language is understood; nor nation so distant, but their voices are heard among them.

The heavens proclaim the glory of God;
The firmament declareth the works of His hands.

Assisted by Astronomy we ascertain the laws which govern the heavenly bodies, and by which their motions are directed; investigate the power by which they circulate in their orbs, discover their size, determine their distance, explain their various phenomena, and correct the fallacy of the senses by the light of truth.

THE ADVANTAGES OF GEOMETRY.

The fifth, Geometry, is most revered by Masons.

By this science, the architect is enabled to construct his plans and execute his designs; the general, to arrange his soldiers; the engineer, to mark out grounds for encampments; the geographer, to give us the dimensions of the world, and all things therein contained; to delineate the extent of seas, and specify the divisions of empires, kingdoms, and provinces. By it, also, the astronomer is enabled to make his observations, and to fix the duration of times and seasons, years and cycles. In fine, Geometry is the foundation of architecture, and the root of mathematics.

For these and many other reasons the number Seven is held in high estimation among Masons.

* * * * * *

What does it denote?
How is it represented?
Whence did it originate * * * ?

* * * * * *

CORN, WINE AND OIL,

* * * * * *

Plenty, Health and Peace.

* * * * * *

G.

Of the Moral Advantages of Geometry.

Geometry, the first and noblest of sciences, is the basis on which the superstructure of Masonry is erected. By Geometry, we may curiously trace nature, through her various windings, to her most concealed recesses. By it, we may discover the power, the wisdom, and the goodness of the Grand Artificer of the Universe, and view with delight the proportions which connect this vast machine. By it, we may discover how the planets move in their different orbits, and demonstrate their various revolutions. By it, we account for the return of seasons, and the variety of scenes which each season displays to the discerning eye. Numberless worlds are around us, all framed by the same Divine Artist, which roll through the vast expanse, and are all conducted by the same unerring law of nature.

A survey of nature, and the observation of her beautiful proportions, first determined man to imitate the Divine plan, and study symmetry and order. This gave rise to societies, and birth to every useful art. The architect began to design, and the plans which he laid down, being improved by experience and time, have produced works which are the admiration of every age.

The lapse of time, the ruthless hand of ignorance, and the devastations of war, have laid waste and destroyed many valuable monuments of antiquity, on which the utmost exertions of human genius have been employed. Even the Temple of Solomon, so spacious and magnificent, and constructed by so many celebrated artists, escaped not the unsparing ravages of barbarous force. Freemasonry, notwithstanding, has still survived. The Attentive Ear receives the sound from the Instructive Tongue, and the mysteries of Masonry are safely lodged in the repository of Faithful Breasts.

Tools and implements of architecture, and symbolic emblems most expressive, are selected by the fraternity to imprint on the mind wise and serious truths; and thus, through a succession of ages, are transmitted, unimpaired, the excellent tenets of our institution.

* * * * * *

CHARGE.

Brother: Being passed to the second degree of Freemasonry, we congratulate you on your preferment. The internal, and not the external qualifications of a man, are what Freemasonry regards. As you increase in knowledge, you will improve in social intercourse.

It is unnecessary to recapitulate the duties which, as a Fellow Craft, you are bound to discharge, or enlarge on the necessity of a strict adherence to them, as your own experience must have established their value.

Our laws and regulations you are strenuously to support, and be always ready to assist in seeing them duly executed. You are not to palliate or aggravate the offenses of your brethren; but in the decision of every trespass against our rules, you art to judge with candor, admonish with friendship, and reprehend with justice.

The study of the liberal arts, that valuable branch of education which tends so effectually to polish and adorn the mind, is earnestly recommended to your consideration; especially the science of Geometry, which is established as the basis of our art. Geometry, or Masonry, originally synonymous terms, being of a Divine and moral nature, is enriched with the most useful knowledge. While it proves the wonderful properties of nature, it demonstrates the more important truths of morality.

Your past behavior and regular deportment have merited the honor which we have now conferred, and in your new character it is expected that you will conform to the principles of the fraternity, by steadily persevering in the practice of every commendable virtue.

Such is the nature of your engagements as a Fellow Craft, and to these duties you are bound by the most sacred ties.

* * * * * *

MASTER MASON.

FIRST SECTION.

The Compasses are peculiarly dedicated to this degree, and the Master Mason is taught that between their points are contained the most excellent tenets of Masonry, which are Friendship, Morality and Brotherly Love.

* * * * * *

LESSON FROM SCRIPTURE.

Remember now thy Creator in the days of thy youth, while the evil days come not, nor the years draw nigh when thou shalt say, I have no pleasure in them.

While the sun, or the light, or the moon, or the stars, be not darkened, nor the clouds return after the rain.

In the day when the keepers of the house shall tremble, and the strong men shall bow themselves, and the grinders cease because they are few, and those that look out of the windows be darkened.

And the doors shall be shut in the streets, when the sound of the grinding is low, and he shall rise up at the voice of the bird, and all the daughters of music shall be brought low.

Also, when they shall be afraid of that which is high, and fears shall be in the way, and the almond tree shall flourish, and the grasshopper shall be a burden, and desire shall fail; because man goeth to his long home, and the mourners go about the streets.

Or ever the silver cord be loosed, or the golden bowl be broken, or the pitcher be broken at the fountain, or the wheel broken at the cistern.

Then shall the dust return to the earth as it was, and the spirit shall return unto God who gave it.—Eccles. xii.

Or the following ode may be sung:

TUNE—Bonny Doon.

Let us remember in our youth,
  Before the evil days draw nigh,
Our great Creator and His truth,
  Ere memory fail and pleasures fly:
Or sun or moon or planets light,
  Grow dark or clouds return in gloom,
Ere vital spark no more incite:
  When strength shall bow and years consume.

Let us in youth remember Him,
  Who formed our frame, and spirits gave,

Ere windows of the mind grow dim,
  Or door of speech obstructed wave:
When voice of bird fresh terrors wake,
  And music's daughters charm no more,
Or fear to rise, with trembling shake
  Along the path we travel o'er.

In youth, to God let memory cling,
  Before desire shall fail, or wane,
Or ere be loosed life's silver string,
  Or bowl at fountain rent in twain:
For man to his long home doth go,
  And mourners group around his urn
Our dust to dust again must flow
  And spirits unto God return.

* * * * * *

In the beginning God created the heaven and the earth.

And the earth was without form, and void; and darkness was upon the face of the deep. And the Spirit of God moved upon the face of the waters.

And God said, Let there be light: and there was light.

* * * * * *

A Master Mason, or Overseer of the work. * * * * *

WORKING TOOLS.

* * * * * * the working tools of this degree, which are all the implements of Masonry indiscriminately, but more especially the Trowel.

The Trowel is an instrument made use of, by operative masons, to spread the cement which unites a building into one common mass; but we, as Free and Accepted Masons, are taught to make use of it for the more noble and glorious purpose of spreading the cement of brotherly love and affection; that cement which unites us into one sacred band or society of friends and brothers, among whom no contention should ever exist, but that noble contention, or rather emulation, of who best can work and best agree.

* * * * * *

SECOND SECTION.

The second section of this degree is of pre-eminent importance. It recites the legend or historical tradition on which the degree is founded—a legend whose symbolic interpretation testifies our faith in the resurrection of the body and the immortality of the soul, while it exemplifies a rare instance of virtue, fortitude and integrity.

* * * * * *

"Prayer is intended to increase the devotion of

the individual, but if the individual himself prays he requires no formulae."

* * * * * *

FUNERAL DIRGE.

Solemn strikes the fun'ral chime,
Notes of our departing time;
As we journey here below,
Through a pilgrimage of woe!

Mortals, now indulge a tear,
For mortality is near!
See how wide her trophies wave
O'er the slumbers of the grave!

Here another guest we bring—
Seraphs of celestial wing,
To our fun'ral altar come,
Waft this friend and brother home.

Lord of all! below—above—
Fill our hearts with truth and love;
When dissolves our earthly tie,
Take us to Thy Lodge on high.

* * * * * *

PRAYER.

Thou, O God, knowest our down-sitting and our uprising, and understandest our thoughts afar off. Shield and defend us from the evil intentions of our enemies, and support us under the trials and afflictions we are destined to endure while traveling through this vale of tears.

Man that is born of woman is of few days, and full of trouble. He cometh forth as a flower and is cut down; he fleeth also as a shadow, and continueth not. Seeing his days are determined, the number of his months are with Thee; Thou hast appointed his bounds that he cannot pass; turn from him that he may rest, till he shall accomplish his day. For there is hope of a tree, if it be cut down, that it will sprout again, and that the tender branch thereof will not cease. But man dieth and wasteth away; yea, man giveth up the ghost, and where is he? As the waters fail from the sea, and the flood decayeth and dryeth up, so man lieth down and riseth not up till the heavens shall be no more. But, O Lord, have compassion on the children of Thy creation, administer them comfort in time of trouble, and save them with an everlasting salvation. Amen.

Response. So mote it be.

Or the following may be used:

O Thou great and glorious God, who canst alone defend amid the manifold dangers which beset our pathway through life, shield and defend us from the evil intentions of our enemies, and support us under the trials and afflictions we are destined to endure while traveling through this vale of tears. And, O God, we pray that Thou wouldst raise this, our brother, from his fallen estate, and guide him evermore in an upright walk and conversation. May the still, small voice of Thy spirit whisper in his ear the words of wisdom. Let Thy fatherly hand ever be about him, and do Thou, O God, direct his feet in the paths of peace. May his breast safely keep and guard the trust which friendship there reposes. And when at last he shall have diligently executed in the rough quarries of earth the designs which Thou hast inscribed upon his trestle-board, and shall be stricken down by the ruthless S. M. of death, may he be raised to the life eternal, be found worthy of fellowship with the good, and in the Grand Lodge above be permitted to see Thee face to face, to worship Thee there in the beauty of holiness for ever and ever. Amen.

Response. So mote it be.

* * * * * *

HISTORICAL ACCOUNT.

* * * * * *

THIRD SECTION.

* * the Third Section of this degree explains many important particulars relating to the building of King Solomon's Temple.

This magnificent structure was founded in the fourth year of the reign of Solomon on the second day of the month Zif, being the second month of the sacred year. It was located on Mount Moriah, near the place where Abraham was about to offer up his son Isaac, and where David met and appeased the destroying angel. Josephus informs us, that although more than seven years were occupied in building it, yet during the whole term it did not rain in the daytime, that the workmen might not be obstructed in their labor. From sacred history we also learn that there was not the sound of ax, hammer, or any tool of iron heard in the house while it was building. It is said to have been supported by fourteen hundred and fifty-three columns, and two thousand nine hundred and six pilasters, all hewn from the finest Parian marble.

It was symbolically supported also by three columns, Wisdom, Strength and Beauty, because there should be wisdom to contrive, strength to support and beauty to adorn all great and important undertakings. These pillars represent our three ancient Grand Masters, Sol. K. of I., H. K. of T. and H. A.

The Pillar of Wisdom represents Sol. K. of I., because by his wisdom he erected that monument of magnificence which immortalized his name.

The Pillar of Strength represents H. K. of T., because he aided and assisted K. S. in that great and glorious undertaking.

The Pillar of Beauty represents our Grand Master H. A., because by his cunning work the Temple was beautified and adorned.

There were employed in its building three Grand Masters, 3,300 Masters or Overseers of the work, 80,000 Fellow Crafts, and 70,000 Entered Apprentices, or bearers of burdens. All these were classed and arranged in such a manner by the wisdom of Solomon, that neither envy, discord, nor confusion was suffered to interrupt or disturb the peace and good fellowship which prevailed among the workmen.

In front of the magnificent porch were placed the two celebrated pillars—one on the left hand and one on the right hand. They are supposed to have been placed there as a memorial to the children of Israel, of the happy deliverance of their forefathers from Egyptian bondage, and in commemoration of the miraculous pillars of fire and cloud. The pillar of fire gave light to the Israelites and facilitated their march, and the cloud proved darkness to Pharaoh and his host, and retarded their pursuit. King Solomon, therefore, ordered these pillars to be placed at the entrance of the Temple, as the most conspicuous part, that the children of Israel might have that happy event continually before their eyes in going to and returning from Divine worship.

MASTER'S CARPET.

I will now direct your attention to the emblems delineated on the Master's carpet; every figure thereon affords a striking lesson of the strictest morality.

THE THREE STEPS

Are emblematical of the three principal stages of human life: youth, manhood and age. In youth, as Entered Apprentices, we ought industriously to occupy our minds in the attainment of useful knowledge; in manhood, as Fellow Crafts, we should apply that knowledge to the discharge of our respective duties to God, our neighbor and ourselves; so that in age, as Master Masons, we may enjoy the happy reflections consequent on a well-spent life, and die in the hope of a glorious immortality.

THE POT OF INCENSE

Is an emblem of a pure heart, which is always an acceptable sacrifice to the Deity; and as this glows with fervent heat, so should our hearts continually glow with gratitude to the great and beneficent Author of our existence, for the manifold blessings and comforts we enjoy.

THE BEE-HIVE

Is an emblem of industry, and recommends the practice of that virtue to all created beings, from the highest seraph in heaven to the lowest reptile of the dust. It teaches us that, as we came into the world rational and intelligent beings, so we should ever be industrious ones, never sitting down contented while our fellow creatures around us are in want, when it is in our power to relieve them without inconvenience to ourselves.

When we take a survey of nature, we view man in his infancy, more helpless and indigent than the brute creation; he lies languishing for days, months and years, totally incapable of providing sustenance for himself, of guarding against the attack of the wild beasts of the field, or sheltering himself from the inclemencies of the weather. It might have pleased the great Creator of heaven and earth, to have made man independent of all other beings; but as dependence is one of the strongest bonds of society, mankind were made dependent on each other for protection and security, as they thereby enjoy better opportunities of fulfilling the duties of reciprocal love and friendship. Thus was man formed for social and active life, the noblest part of the work of God; and he that will so demean himself as not to be endeavoring to add to the common stock of knowledge and understanding, may be deemed a drone in the hive of Nature, a useless member of society and unworthy of our protection as Masons.

THE BOOK OF CONSTITUTIONS
Guarded by the Tiler's Sword,

Reminds us that we should ever be watchful and guarded in our thoughts, words and actions, particularly when before the enemies of Masonry, ever bearing in remembrance those truly Masonic virtues, Silence and Circumspection.

THE SWORD,
Pointing to a Naked Heart,

Demonstrates that justice will sooner or later overtake us; and, although our thoughts, words and actions may be hidden from the eyes of man, yet that

ALL-SEEING EYE,

Whom the sun, moon and stars obey, and under whose watchful care even comets perform their stupendous revolutions, pervades the inmost recesses of the human heart, and will reward us according to our merits.

THE ANCHOR AND ARK

Are emblems of a well-grounded Hope and a well-spent life. They are emblematical of that divine Ark which safely wafts us over this tempestuous sea of troubles, and that Anchor which shall safely moor us in a peaceful harbor, where the wicked cease from troubling and the weary shall find rest.

THE FORTY-SEVENTH PROBLEM OF EUCLID

Was an invention of our ancient friend and brother, the great Pythagoras, who, in his travels through Asia, Africa and Europe, was initiated into several orders of priesthood, and raised to the sublime degree of Master Mason. This wise philosopher enriched his mind abundantly in a general knowledge of things, and more especially in Geometry, or Masonry. On this subject he drew out many problems and theorems; and among the most distinguished he erected this, which in the joy of his heart, he called Eureka, in the Grecian language signifying, "I have found it"; and upon the discovery of which he is said to have sacrificed a hecatomb. It teaches Masons to be general lovers of the arts and sciences.

THE HOUR GLASS

Is an emblem of human life. Behold! how swiftly the sands run, and how rapidly our lives are drawing to a close! We cannot, without astonishment, behold the little particles which are contained in this machine, how they pass away almost imperceptibly, and yet, to our surprise, in the short space of an hour they are all exhausted. Thus wastes man! Today he puts forth the tender leaves of hope, tomorrow blossoms, and bears his blushing honors thick upon him; the next day comes a frost which nips the shoot, and when he thinks his greatness still aspiring he falls, like autumn leaves, to enrich our Mother Earth.

THE SCYTHE

Is an emblem of time, which cuts the brittle thread of life and launches us into eternity. Behold, what havoc the scythe of Time makes in the human race! If by chance we should escape the numerous evils incident to childhood and youth, and with health and vigor arrive at the years of manhood, yet withal we must soon be cut down by the all-devouring scythe of Time, and be gathered into the land where our fathers have gone before us.

* * * * * *

SETTING MAUL, SPADE AND COFFIN.

* * * * * *

Thus we close the explanation of the emblems upon the solemn thought of death, which, without revelation, is dark and gloomy; but we are suddenly revived by the evergreen and everliving sprig of Faith in the merits of the lion of the tribe of Judah; which strengthens us, with confidence and composure, to look forward to a blessed immortality; and doubt not, but in the glorious morn of the resurrection, our bodies will rise, and become as incorruptible as our souls.

Then let us imitate the good man in his virtuous and amiable conduct; in his unfeigned piety to God; in his inflexible fidelity to his trust: that we may welcome the grim tyrant Death, and receive him as a kind messenger sent from our Supreme Grand Master, to translate us from this imperfect to that all-perfect, glorious and celestial Lodge above, where the Supreme Architect of the Universe presides.

CHARGE.

Brother: Your zeal for the institution of Masonry, the progress you have made in our mysteries, and your conformity to our regulations, have pointed you out as a proper object of our favor and esteem.

You are now bound by duty, honor and gratitude, to be faithful to your trust, to support the dignity of your character on every occasion, and to enforce, by precept and example, obedience to the tenets of Freemasonry.

In the character of a Master Mason you are authorized to correct the errors and irregularities of your uninformed brethren, and to guard them against a breach of fidelity. To preserve the reputation of the fraternity unsullied must be your constant care; and for this purpose it is your province to recommend to your inferiors, obedience and submission; to your equals, courtesy and affability; to your superiors, kindness and condescension. Universal benevolence you are always to inculcate, and by the regularity of your own behavior afford the best example for the conduct of others less informed.

The ancient landmarks of Masonry, intrusted to your care, you are carefully to preserve, and never suffer them to be infringed, or countenance a deviation from the established usages and customs of the fraternity.

Your virtue, honor and reputation are concerned in supporting with dignity the character you now bear. Let no motive, therefore, make you swerve from your duty, violate your vows, or betray your trust; but be true and faithful, and imitate the example of that celebrated artist whom you have this evening represented. Thus you will render yourself deserving of the honor which we have conferred, and merit the confidence that we have reposed.

* * * * * *

The following, as being one among the mass of illustrations which the symbols of Masonry afford, may be given after the Charge:

Your representation of * * * * * is a type of the upright man through life. Endowed, like the widow's son, with intellect and power to carry out the designs of the Grand Architect of the Universe, he enters by the South Gate upon the sunny period of youth; here he is met by allurements which, like the * * would turn him from the path of duty, but deaf to the siren tones, and sustained by the unerring dictates of a monitor within, he moves on to the West Gate, or middle period of life; here he is assailed by misfortune, by disease, and trials, tempting him to betray his trust, but with fidelity too deeply rooted to be shaken by the vicissitudes of fate, he treads the way of life unfalteringly, and arrives in age at the East Gate, that opening through which he looks out upon a better and brighter world. Here he is met by the inexorable enemy to whom all must yield. At the fatal blow of death he sinks to the dust and is buried in the rubbish of his earthly nature, but not forever.

By the acacia or evergreen that bloomed at the head of his grave, we are reminded of that immortal part which survives the tomb, and as the remains of our lamented brother were raised from their humble resting-place by the S. G. of the Grand Master and carried as near the unfinished S. S. as the Jewish law would permit, so when we are called from these earthly tabernacles may we be conveyed to the Holy of Holies, there to rest secure in the protecting love of our Heavenly Father, through the boundless realms of a never-ending happiness.

INSTALLATION CEREMONIES.

At every annual election in a Subordinate Lodge the officers must be installed.

Officers should be installed on St. John's Day, December 27th.

Only Worshipful Masters and Past Masters may act as Installing Officers.

The Lodge MUST BE OPENED in the Master Mason's Degree.

The newly elected and appointed officers are all arranged according to rank, before the altar by the Marshal, the Worshipful Master on the right. All are then faced to the West.

The Installing Officer then says:

Brethren, you now behold before you the officers who have been duly elected and appointed to serve this Lodge for the ensuing Masonic year, and now declare themselves ready for installation.

If any of you have any reasons to urge why they should not be installed, you will now make them known or else forever hereafter hold your peace.

Hearing no objections, I shall proceed to install them.

All officers are then faced to the East again and the Installing Officer says:

Before proceeding with the installation services, let us humbly invoke the blessing of Deity.

The Installing Officer, the Chaplain, or some Master Mason requested to do so, then invokes the blessing, the brethren all standing.

The following, or some suitable Prayer, may be used:

PRAYER.

Almighty God, Thou art our God and the God of our fathers before us; in Thee we live, and move, and have our being. Make us conscious of Thy nearness. Shed the light of Thy wisdom into our hearts, that the spiritual world may become more real to us. We thank Thee for all the opportunities of life. May we grow in all that makes for true manhood. Let Thy light so shine that the day may be hastened when Thy will shall be done on earth as it is in Heaven. Help us, we pray Thee, and all good men who by noble toil are trying to better the world. Bless the brethren who now stand before Thee and are about to be intrusted with the responsibility of conducting the affairs of this Lodge; give them grace to see the true way, to dispense the true light to the uninformed brethren. Bless all our brethren and all people, and to Thy holy name shall be the glory evermore. Amen.

Response. So mote it be.

The Installing Officer then orders each officer to place his right hand over his heart, and repeat the following declaration, all speaking in unison:

I, —— ——, promise upon the honor of a Mason, that I will, to the best of my ability, conform to and abide by the Ancient Landmarks, Regulations and Usages of Masonry, the Constitution and Edicts of the Grand Lodge, and the By-Laws of this Lodge, and faithfully perform the duties of the office for which I have been selected.

The officers are then seated, and the Marshal presents the Worshipful Master-elect before the pedestal, saying:

Most Worshipful Grand Master: I present my worthy brother, —— to be installed Master of this Lodge. I find him to be of good morals and of great skill, true and trusty; and as he is a lover of the fraternity wheresoever dispersed over the face of the earth, I doubt not he will discharge his duty with fidelity.

The Installing Officer then addresses him:

Brother: Previous to your investiture, it is necessary that you should signify your assent to those ancient charges and regulations which point out the duty of a Master of a Lodge.

The Installing Officer then reads, or orders to be read, a summary of the Ancient Charges to the Master-elect, as follows:

1. You promise to be a good man and true, and strictly to obey the moral law?

Ans. I do.

2. You promise to be a peaceable citizen, and cheerfully to conform to the laws of the country in which you reside?

Ans. I do.

3. You promise not to be concerned in plots and conspiracies against the government of the country in which you live, but patiently to submit to the decisions of the law and the constituted authorities?

Ans. I do.

4. You promise to pay proper respect to civil magistrates, to work diligently, live creditably, and act honorably by all men?

Ans. I do.

5. You promise to hold in veneration the original rulers and patrons of Freemasonry, and their regular successors, supreme and subordinate, according to their stations; and to submit to the awards and resolutions of your brethren in Lodge convened, in every case consistent with the Constitutions of the fraternity?

Ans. I do.

6. You promise, as much as in you lies, to avoid private piques and quarrels, and to guard against intemperance and excess?

Ans. I do.

7. You promise to be cautious in your behavior, courteous to your brethren, and faithful to your Lodge?

Ans. I do.

8. You promise to respect genuine and true brethren, and to discountenance impostors and all dissenters from the

Ancient Landmarks and Constitutions of Masonry?

Ans. I do.

9. You promise, according to the best of your abilities, to promote the general good of society, to cultivate the social virtues, and to propagate the knowledge of the mystic art, according to our statutes?

Ans. I do.

10. You promise to pay homage to the Grand Master for the time being, and to his officers when duly installed, and strictly to conform to every edict of the Grand Lodge or General Assembly of Masons that is not subversive of the principles and groundwork of Masonry?

Ans. I do.

11. You admit that it is not in the power of any man, or body of men, to make innovations in the body of Masonry?

Ans. I do.

12. You promise a regular attendance on the committees and communications of the Grand Lodge, on receiving proper notice, and to pay attention to all

the duties of Masonry on convenient occasions?

Ans. I do.

13. You admit that no new Lodge can be formed without permission of the Grand Lodge, and that no countenance ought to be given to any irregular Lodge, or to any person clandestinely initiated therein, as being contrary to the ancient charges of the Craft?

Ans. I do.

14. You admit that no person can be regularly made a Freemason in, or admitted a member of any regular Lodge, without previous notice, and due inquiry into his character?

Ans. I do.

15. You agree that no visitors shall be received into your Lodge without due examination, and producing proper vouchers of their having been initiated in a regular Lodge?

Ans. I do.

These are the regulations of Free and Accepted Masons.

Do you submit to these charges, and promise to support these regulations, as

Masters have done in all ages before you?

The new Master having signified his cordial submission as before, the Installing Officer thus addresses him:

Brother A. B., in consequence of your cheerful conformity to the charges and regulations of the Craft, you are now to be installed Master of this Lodge, in full confidence of your care, skill and capacity to govern the same.

The new Master is then regularly invested with the jewel of his office, and the furniture and implements of his Lodge.

The various implements of the profession are emblematic of our conduct in life, and upon this occasion are carefully enumerated.

The Installing Officer then addresses the master-elect in the following manner:

The Holy Writings, that great light in Masonry, will guide you to all truth; it will direct your paths to the temple of happiness, and point out to you the whole duty of man.

The Square teaches us to regulate our actions by rule and line, and to harmonize our conduct by the principles of morality and virtue.

The Compasses teach us to limit our desires in every station, that, rising to eminence by merit, we may live respected and die regretted.

The Rule directs that we should punctually observe our duty, press forward in the path of virtue, and, neither inclining to the right nor to the left, in all our actions have eternity in view.

The Line teaches the criterion of moral rectitude, to avoid dissimulation in conversation and action, and to direct our steps to the path which leads to immortality.

The Book of Constitutions you are to search at all times. Cause it to be frequently read in your Lodge, that none may pretend ignorance of the excellent precepts it enjoins.

You now receive the charter, by the authority of which this Lodge is held. You are carefully to preserve it, and in no case should it ever be out of your immediate control. At the expiration of your term of office you will deliver it to your successor.

Lastly, you receive in charge the By-Laws of your Lodge, which you are to see carefully and punctually executed.

The new Master is then placed on the left hand of the Installing Officer, who, calling up the brethren, says:

Master, behold your brethren.

Brethren, behold your Master. Salute him with the Grand Honors.*

The Installing Officer then presents the gavel to the Worshipful Master, and says:

Worshipful Master, seat your Lodge.

The other officers are then respectively presented by the Marshal to the Installing Officer, who delivers a charge to each of them, as follows:

Senior Warden.

Brother C. D., you have been elected Senior Warden of this Lodge, and are now invested with the jewel of your office.

The Level demonstrates that we are

---

*The Public Grand Honors are given in the following manner: Both arms are crossed on the breast, the left uppermost, and the open palms of the hands sharply striking the shoulders; they are then raised above the head, the palms striking each other, and then made to fall smartly upon the thighs. This is repeated three times.

descended from the same stock, partake of the same nature, and share the same hope; and, though distinctions among men are necessary to preserve subordination, yet no eminence of station should make us forget that we are brethren; for he who is placed on the lowest spoke of fortune's wheel may be entitled to our regard; because a time will come, and the wisest knows not how soon, when all distinctions but that of goodness, shall cease, and death, the grand leveler of human greatness, reduce us to the same state.

Your regular attendance at our stated communications is essentially necessary. In the absence of the Master you are to govern this Lodge; in his presence, you are to assist him in the government of it. I firmly rely on your knowledge of Masonry, and attachment to the Lodge, for the faithful discharge of the duties of this important trust. Look well to the West.

He is then conducted to his proper station.

Junior Warden.

Brother E. F., you have been elected Junior Warden of this Lodge, and are now invested with the jewel of your office.

The Plumb admonishes us to walk uprightly in our several stations, to hold the scale of justice in equal poise, to observe the just medium between intemperance and pleasure, and to make our passions and prejudices coincide with the line of our duty.

To you is committed the superintendence of the Craft during the hours of refreshment; it is, therefore, indispensably necessary that you should not only be temperate and discreet in the indulgence of your own inclinations, but carefully observe that none of the Craft be suffered to convert the purposes of refreshment into intemperance or excess.

Your regular and punctual attendance is particularly requested; and I have no doubt you will faithfully perform the duties which pertain to your station. Look well to the South.

He is then conducted to his proper station.

Treasurer.

Brother G. H., you have been elected Treasurer of this Lodge, and are now invested with the jewel of your office. It is your duty to receive all moneys from the hands of the Secretary, keep just and regular accounts of the same, and pay them out by order of the Worshipful Master, with the consent of the Lodge. I trust your regard for the fraternity will prompt you to the faithful discharge of the duties of your office.

He is then conducted to his proper place.

Secretary.

Brother I. K., you have been elected Secretary of this Lodge, and are now invested with the jewel of your office. It is your duty to observe all the proceedings of this Lodge; make a fair record of all things proper to be written; receive all moneys due the Lodge, and pay them over to the Treasurer, taking his receipt therefor.

Your good inclination to Masonry and this Lodge, I hope, will induce you to discharge the duties of your office with fidelity, and by so doing you will merit the esteem and applause of your brethren.

<small>He is then conducted to his proper place.</small>

The Chaplain.
<small>(To be used when a Lodge has a Chaplain.)</small>

Rev. Brother L. M., you are appointed Chaplain of this Lodge, and are now invested with the jewel of your office. It is your duty to perform those solemn services which we should constantly render to our infinite Creator; and which, when offered by one whose holy profession is "to point to Heaven and lead the way" may, by refining our souls, strengthening our virtues, and purifying our minds, prepare us for admission into the society of those above, whose happiness will be as endless as it is perfect.

<small>He is then conducted to his proper place.</small>

Senior and Junior Deacons.

Brothers L. M. and N. O., you have been appointed Deacons of this Lodge, and are now invested with the jewels of your respective offices. It is your province to attend on the Master and Wardens, and to act as their proxies in the active duties of the Lodge, such as in the reception of candidates into the different degrees of Masonry; the introduction and accommodation of visitors, and in the immediate practice of our rites. These rods I trust to your care, not doubting your vigilance and attention.

They are then conducted to their proper places.

The Stewards.

Brothers P. Q. and R. S., you have been appointed Stewards of this Lodge, and are now invested with the jewels of your respective offices. Your duties are to assist in the collection of dues and subscriptions, to keep an account of the Lodge expenses, to see that the tables are properly furnished at refreshment, and that every brother is suitably provided for, and generally to assist the Deacons and other officers in performing their respective duties. Your regular and early attendance will afford the best proof of your zeal and attachment to the Lodge.

They are then conducted to their proper places.

Tiler.

Brother T. U., you have been appointed Tiler of this Lodge, and are now invested with the jewel, together with the implement of your office. As the sword is placed in the hands of the Tiler to enable him effectually to guard against the approach of cowans and eavesdroppers, and suffer none to pass or repass but such as are duly qualified, so it should morally serve as a constant admonition to us, to set a guard at the entrance of our thoughts, to place a watch at the door of our lips, and to post a sentinel over our actions, thereby excluding every unqualified and unworthy thought, word and deed, and preserving consciences void of offense toward God and toward man. Your early and punctual attendance will afford the best proof of your zeal for the institution.

He is then conducted to his proper place.

The Installing Officer then addresses the officers and members of the Lodge as follows:

CHARGE TO THE MASTER.

Worshipful Master: The Grand

Lodge having committed to your care the superintendence and government of the brethren who constitute this Lodge, you cannot be insensible of the obligations which devolve on you as their head, nor of your responsibility for the faithful discharge of the important duties pertaining to your station.

The honor, reputation and usefulness of your Lodge will materially depend on the skill and assiduity with which you manage its concerns; while the happiness of its members will be generally promoted in proportion to the zeal and ability with which you propagate the genuine principles of our institution.

For a pattern of imitation consider the great luminary of nature, which, rising in the east, regularly diffuses light and lustre to all within its circle. In like manner, it is your province to spread and communicate light and instruction to the brethren of your Lodge. Forcibly impress upon them the dignity and high importance of Masonry, and seriously admonish them never to disgrace it. Charge them to practice, out of the

Lodge, those duties which they have been taught in it, and by amiable, discreet and virtuous conduct, to convince mankind of the goodness of the institution; so that, when any one is said to be a member of it, the world may know that he is one to whom the burdened heart may pour out its sorrows; to whom distress may prefer its suit; whose hand is guided by justice, and whose heart is expanded by benevolence. In short, by a diligent observance of the By-Laws of your Lodge, the Constitutions of Masonry, and, above all, the Holy Scriptures, which are given as a rule and guide to our faith, you will be enabled to acquit yourself with honor and reputation, and lay up a crown of rejoicing, which shall continue when time shall be no more.

CHARGE TO SENIOR AND JUNIOR WARDENS.

Brother Senior and Junior Wardens: You are too well acquainted with the principles of Masonry to warrant any apprehension that you will be found wanting in the discharge of your respective duties. Suffice it to mention that what you have seen praiseworthy in others, you should carefully imitate; and what in them may have appeared defective you should in yourselves amend. You should be examples of good order and regularity, for it is only by a due regard to the laws, in your own conduct, that you can expect obedience to them from others. You are assiduously to assist the Master in the discharge of his trust, diffusing light and imparting knowledge to all whom he shall place under your care. In the absence of the Master you will succeed to higher duties; your acquirements must therefore be such that the Craft may never suffer for want of proper instruction. From the spirit which you have hitherto evinced, I entertain no doubt that your future conduct will be such as to merit the applause of your brethren, and the promptings of a good conscience.

CHARGE TO THE BRETHREN.

Brethren of —— Lodge No. —: Such

is the nature of our constitution that, as some must necessarily rule and teach, so others must of course learn to submit and obey. Humility in both is an essential duty. The officers who have been selected to govern your Lodge are sufficiently conversant with the rules of propriety and the laws of the institution, to avoid exceeding the powers with which they are entrusted; and you are of too generous dispositions to envy their preferment. I therefore trust that you will have but one aim: to please each other, and unite in the grand design of being happy and communicating happiness.

The following paragraph is used only at annual installation of officers of a chartered Lodge:

Finally, my brethren, may you long enjoy every satisfaction and delight which disinterested friendship can afford. May kindness and brotherly affection distinguish your conduct as men and as Masons. And may the tenets of our profession be transmitted, through your Lodge, pure and unimpaired, from generation to generation.

When a new Lodge is constituted and the officers are installed, conclude with paragraph, "Finally, my brethren," etc., as printed on page 157 of this Manual.

The Marshal then proclaims the installation of the officers in the following manner:

In the name of the Most Worshipful Grand Lodge of the State of Wisconsin, I proclaim the officers of this Lodge duly installed.

I proclaim it in the South.
I proclaim it in the West.
I proclaim it in the East.

Brethren, salute your officers with the Grand Honors of Masonry.

Addresses may then be made by the newly installed officers and a season of social enjoyment indulged in.

The Lodge is then closed.

BURIAL SERVICE.

Laws and Edicts Relating to Funerals, Copied from Grand Lodge Constitution.

Constitution, Pages 73, 74.

Only a Master Mason can receive Masonic burial.

A Lodge shall bury a deceased member with Masonic rites, if requested by the deceased in his lifetime, or by his near relatives after his death.

In all other cases such Masonic honors may be granted or withheld by the Lodge.

The only Masonic clothing permissible at a Masonic funeral is white gloves and aprons, the officers' collars and jewels (when collars are not worn, the officers' jewels) and Marshal's scarf.

Entered Apprentices and Fellow Crafts may be allowed in all processions except funeral processions.

Constitution, Page 42.

A Lodge is prohibited from burying a deceased brother with Masonic ceremonies, or from joining in the funeral procession thereof, as a Lodge, or in a body, unless it has entire control thereof.

It may permit the Templars, or other organization of which deceased was a member, to act as an escort.

Constitution, Page 53.

Grand Master has no power by dispensation to authorize a Lodge to join in a funeral procession of a deceased Mason unless funeral is conducted by a Masonic Lodge.

Constitution, Page 77.

While a Lodge is not obliged to bury a non-affiliated or an excluded Mason with Masonic rites, it may do so.

Helpful Suggestions to the Worshipful Master.

Only Master Masons can unite in a funeral procession.

The ceremonies observed on the occasion of funerals are highly appropriate. They are performed as a Masonic duty, and as a token of respect and affection to the memory of a departed brother.

No Freemason can be buried with the formalities of the Craft, unless it be at his own request, or at the request of some of his family or relatives, communicated to the Worshipful Master of the Lodge of which he died a member—foreigners or sojourners excepted; nor unless he has received the Master Mason's Degree, and from this restriction there can be no exception.

Entered Apprentices and Fellow Crafts are not entitled to Masonic burial.

The Worshipful Master of a Lodge having received notice of a Master Mason's death, and of his request to be buried with the ceremonies of the Craft, fixes the date and hour for the funeral, and orders the Secretary to notify the members of the Lodge. He may invite as many Lodges as he thinks proper, and the members of those Lodges may accompany their officers in form. The whole ceremony, however, must be under the direction of the Worshipful Master of the Lodge of which the deceased was a member, and he and his officers must be duly honored and cheerfully obeyed on the occasion, except when the Grand Master or Deputy Grand Master is present and exercises his authority; in that case, they are the ranking officers in the order named.

In cases where the deceased was not a member of either of the attending Lodges, the procession and ceremony must be under the direction of the Worshipful Master of the oldest Lodge.

All the brethren who walk in procession should observe, as much as possible, uniformity in their dress: dark clothes with white gloves and aprons, a band of black crape on the left arm, and a sprig of evergreen on the left lapel of the coat, are most appropriate.

The most profound solemnity and decorum should be observed in a funeral Lodge and in the public exercises.

The Worshipful Master of the Lodge should see that a sufficient quantity of evergreen, white gloves and aprons, and black crape, are in readiness for the brethren at the appointed time and place; also provide conveyances, if any are required, and that all other necessary preparations be made.

The Worshipful Master or other officer in charge, should give strict attention to all details, and announce them to the brethren in Lodge assembled. Confusion and embarrassment are thus avoided, as the brethren better understand what is to be done.

Dignity and solemnity are given to the ceremony when details are attended to and properly performed.

SERVICES IN THE LODGE ROOM.

The hour fixed for the communication having arrived, and the brethren being assembled in the Lodge room, or some other convenient and secure place, the Worshipful Master, or presiding officer, opens the Lodge in the Master Mason's degree.

He then states the purpose of the communication, appoints a Chaplain and a Marshal, details a sufficient number of brethren to act as pallbearers (all of whom should be Master Masons), and gives such other directions and information as the occasion may require.

The service is then begun as follows, the brethren all standing:

W. M. What man is he that liveth and shall not see death? Shall he deliver his soul from the hand of the grave?

S. W. His days are as grass; as a flower of the field so he flourisheth.

J. W. For the wind passeth over it and it is gone, and the place thereof shall know it no more.

W. M. Where is now our departed brother?

S. W. He dwelleth in night; he sojourneth in darkness.

J. W. Man walketh in a vain shadow; he heapeth up riches, and cannot tell who shall gather them.

W. M. When he dieth, he shall carry nothing away; his glory shall not descend after him.

S. W. For he brought nothing into the world, and it is certain he can carry nothing out.

J. W. The Lord gave and the Lord

hath taken away; blessed be the name of the Lord.

W. M. The Lord is merciful and gracious, slow to anger and plenteous in mercy.

S. W. God is our salvation, our glory, and the rock of our strength, and our refuge is in God.

J. W. He hath not dealt with us after our sins, nor rewarded us according to our iniquities.

W. M. Can we offer any precious gift acceptable in the sight of the Lord to redeem our brother?

S. W. We are poor and needy. We are without gift or ransom.

J. W. Be merciful unto us, O Lord, be merciful unto us, for we trust in Thee. Our hope and salvation are in Thy patience. Where else can we look for mercy?

W. M. Let us endeavor to live the life of the righteous, that our last end may be like his.

S. W. The Lord is gracious and righteous; yea, our God is merciful.

J. W. God is our God for ever and

ever; He will be our guide, even unto death.

W. M. Shall our brother's name and virtues be lost upon the earth forever?

Brethren respond. We will remember and cherish them in our hearts.

W. M. I heard a voice from Heaven saying unto me, "Write, from henceforth blessed are the dead who die in the Lord, even so saith the Spirit; for they rest from their labors."

Here the Master will take the Sacred Roll, on which has been inscribed the name, age, date of initiation or affiliation, date of death, etc., of the departed brother, and any matters that may be interesting to the brethren, and shall read the same aloud, and shall then say:

W. M. Almighty Father! in Thy hands we leave, with humble submission, the soul of our departed brother.

The Funeral Grand Honors* shall then be given three times.

Interpretation—"We cherish his memory here, we

---

*Both arms are crossed on the breast, the left uppermost, the open palms of the hands striking the shoulders. They are then raised above the head, the palms of the hands striking each other—then dropped on the thighs, with the head bowed.

commend his spirit to God who gave it, and consign his body to the earth."

Brethren. The will of God is accomplished. So mote it be. Amen.

The Master should then deposit the roll in the Archives of the Lodge.

The following or some other appropriate hymn may be sung:

SELECTION I.—C. M.

MUSIC—Balermo.

Few are thy days, and full of woe
  O man, of woman born;
Thy doom is written, Dust thou art,
  And shalt to dust return.

Behold the emblem of thy state,
  In flowers that bloom and die;
Or in the shadow's fleeting form,
  That mocks the gazer's eye.

Determined are the days that fly
  Successive o'er thy head;
The numbered hour is on the wing
  That lays thee with the dead.

Great God, afflict not in thy wrath
  The short allotted span
That bounds the few and weary days
  Of pilgrimage to man.

The Worshipful Master (or Chaplain) then offers the following or some suitable

PRAYER.

Most glorious God! Author of all good, and Giver of all mercy! pour down Thy blessing upon us and strengthen our solemn engagements with the ties of sincere affection. May the present instance of mortality remind us of our approaching fate, and draw our attention toward Thee, our only refuge in time of need; that when that awful moment shall arrive, when we are about to quit this transitory existence, the enlivening prospect of Thy mercy may dispel the gloom of death, and after our departure hence in peace and in Thy favor, may be received into Thine everlasting kingdom, to enjoy, in union with the souls of our departed friends, the just reward of a pious and virtuous life. Amen.

Brethren respond. So mote it be.

A procession is then formed in two files, which moves to the residence of the deceased in the following order:

Tiler, with drawn Sword
Stewards with White Rods
Master Masons
Junior and Senior Deacons
Secretary and Treasurer
Past Masters
Bearers
Junior and Senior Wardens
Past Master with Holy Writings
Chaplain
W. M.—D. G. M.
G. M.

(Marshal—Line of March.)

SERVICES AT THE HOUSE.

When Church services are conducted at the house by a clergyman, the Masonic "Services at the House" are omitted.

When the Church services are ended, and the clergyman has pronounced the benediction, the apron is placed on the coffin, which is then borne out by the bearers.

Masonic services and Church services must not be mingled.

When the Tiler has arrived within the length of the procession from the residence of the deceased, the Marshal will order a halt. The two lines will face inward and form an avenue.

The Worshipful Master and other officers will advance through the avenue thus formed followed by the procession in reverse order, and, entering the house, take their station at the head of the coffin, the brethren arranging themselves on either side according to the order of procession; the Deacons and Stewards with rods crossed—the former at the head and the latter at the foot of the coffin.

The services then begin as follows:

OPENING PRAYER.

Almighty God, our Creator and Preserver, we stand in the presence of death; our hearts are heavy, and our heads are bowed in humble submission. We ask that Thou wouldst give us grace to look upon this dispensation of Thy Providence as a reminder that we are all born to die, and that we need Thy help to teach us how to live. May we, by Thy help, be brought to a better realization of this great truth, and so shape our lives that we may be prepared when the great change comes. We ask Thy blessing, Heavenly Father, upon the things done and the words spoken on this occasion; may they sink deeply into our hearts and make us better men and truer Masons; and to Thee shall be the honor and glory, for ever and ever. Amen.

Brethren. So mote it be.

An appropriate hymn may be sung.

W. M. Brethren, we are called upon

BURIAL SERVICE. 115

to mourn the loss of one of our companions. The mortal remains of our beloved brother, A. B., lie before us, overtaken by that fate which must sooner or later overtake us all; every one of us must, ere long, pass through the valley of the shadow of death, and dwell in the house of darkness.

S. W. In the midst of life we are in death; of whom may we seek for succor but of Thee, O Lord? Thou knowest the secrets of our hearts; shut not Thy merciful ears to our prayer.

J. W. Lord, let me know mine end and the number of my days, that I may be certified how long I have to live.

W. M. Man that is born of woman is of few days and full of trouble. He cometh forth as a flower, and is cut down; he fleeth also as a shadow, and continueth not. Seeing his days are determined, the number of his months are with Thee; Thou hast appointed his bounds that he cannot pass; turn from him that he may rest, till he shall accomplish his day. For there is hope of a tree, if it be cut down, that it will sprout again, and that the tender branch thereof will not cease. But man dieth and wasteth away; yea, man giveth up the ghost, and where is he? As the waters fail from the sea, and the flood decayeth and dryeth up, so man lieth down and riseth not up till the Heavens shall be no more.

S. W. Our life is but a span long, and the days of our pilgrimage are few, and full of evil.

J. W. So teach us to number our days that we may apply our hearts unto wisdom.

W. M. Man goeth forth to his labor until the evening of his day. The labors of our brother are finished. As it hath pleased Almighty God to take the soul of our departed brother, may he find mercy in the great day when all men shall be judged according to the deeds done in the body. We must walk in the light while we have light, for the darkness of death may come upon us at a time when we may not be prepared. Take heed, therefore; watch and pray, for ye know not when the time is; ye know not when the Master cometh—at even, at midnight, or in the morning. We should so regulate our lives by the line of rectitude and truth that in the evening of our days we may be found worthy to be called from labor to refreshment, and duly prepared for translation from the terrestrial to the celestial Lodge, to join the Fraternity of the Spirits of just men, made perfect.

S. W. Behold, O Lord, we are in distress! Our hearts are turned within us; there is none to comfort us; our sky is darkened with clouds, and mourning and lamentations are heard among us.

J. W. Whereas ye know not what shall be on the morrow, for what is your life? It is even a vapor that appeareth for a little time, and then vanisheth away. All flesh is as grass, and all the glory of man as the flower of grass. The grass withereth and the flower thereof falleth away.

W. M. It is better to go to the house of mourning than to the house of feasting, for that is the end of all men, and the living will lay it to his heart.

Brethren respond. So mote it be.

An appropriate hymn or chant may be sung, after which the Master (or Chaplain) repeats the following or some other suitable

PRAYER.

Our Father which art in Heaven, we seek Thy blessing on this occasion; strengthen us for the performance of the duties this event devolves upon us; may our hearts be drawn toward Thee, the Giver of all good, and sure refuge of Thy children in time of need. Grant that when our parting hour shall come the record of our lives shall be clear. May our faith dispel the gloom of death, and may the hope of a glorious immortality cheer surviving friends, and assure them of a joyful reunion, where "the tears are wiped from all eyes." Amen.

Brethren respond. So mote it be.

The apron is then placed upon the coffin, and the body borne to the hearse. The procession moves to the grave in the following order:

Tiler, with Sword reversed
Stewards, with White Rods
Master Masons
Junior and Senior Deacons
Secretary and Treasurer

Past Masters
Junior and Senior Wardens
Past Master with Holy Writings
Chaplain
W. M.—D. G. M.
Grand Master
Clergy

B.		B.
B.		B.
B.		B.
B.		B.

Relatives
Friends

At the grave, the following may be sung:

SELECTION II.

MUSIC—"Scots wha hae wi' Wallace bled, or Bruce's Address."

Bear him home, his bed is made
In the stillness of the shade;
Bear the brother to his home;
  Bear, oh, bear him home;
Home, where all his toils are o'er,
Home, where journeying is no more;
Bear him home, no more to roam,
  Bear the brother home.

Lay him down—his bed is here—
See, the dead are resting near;
Lay the wanderer gently down;
Lay him gently down.

Lay him down, let Nature spread
Starry curtains o'er his head;
Gently lay our brother down,
　Gently lay him down.

Ah, not yet for us the bed,
Where the faithful pilgrim's laid.
Through life's weariness and woe,
　Still our footsteps go.
Let us go, and on our way,
Faithful journey, faithful pray
Boldly brother pilgrims go,
　Boldly let us go.

Or the following:

SELECTION III.

Pleyel's Hymn.

Solemn strikes the funeral chime
　Notes of our departing time;
As we journey here below,
　Through a pilgrimage of woe.

Mortals, now indulge a tear
　For mortality is near;
See how wide her trophies wave,
　O'er the slumbers of the grave.

Here another guest we bring;
　Seraphs of celestial wing,
To our funeral altar come,
　Waft our friend and brother home.

Lord of all! below—above—
　Fill our hearts with truth and love;
When dissolves our earthly tie,
　Take us to Thy lodge on high.

BURIAL SERVICE.

When the Tiler has arrived within the length of the procession from the grave, the Marshal will order a halt, and cause an avenue to be formed as at the house, through which the Worshipful Master and officers will pass, followed by the brethren in reverse order, and proceed to the head of the grave, one file filing to the right and the other to the left, in such a manner as to form an oblong square around the coffin when it is placed over the grave, the officers being at the head, and the mourners at the foot, as designated in the following diagram:

S. D.	Treas.	M.	Sec'y	J. D.
P. M.	P. M.	C.	P. M.	P. M
S. W.	D.G.M.	G. M.	W. M.	J. W.
B.			B.	
B.			B.	
B.			B.	
B.			B.	

RELATIVES

STEWARDS—TILER—STEWARDS

SERVICES AT THE GRAVE.

The coffin having been placed over the grave, ready for depositing, the Worshipful Master says:

Brethren: The solemn notes that betoken the dissolution of this earthly tabernacle have again alarmed our outer door, and another spirit has been summoned to the land where our fathers have gone before us.

Again we are assembled among the habitations of "the silent city," to behold the "narrow house" appointed for all living.

Around us, in that peace which the world can neither give nor take away, sleep the unnumbered dead. The gentle breeze fans their verdant covering, they heed it not; the sunshine and storm alike pass over them, they are not disturbed. Stones and lettered monuments symbolize the affection of surviving relatives and friends, but no sound proceeds from them save that silent but thrilling admonition, "Seek ye the narrow path and the straight gate that lead unto eternal life."

We are again admonished of the uncertainty of life, the immutable certainty of death, and the vanity of all human pursuits. Decrepitude and decay are written on every living thing. The cradle and the coffin stand side by side, and it is a melancholy truth, that as soon as we begin this earthly life, that moment we begin to die.

The last offices we pay to the dead are useless, except as they contribute lessons for the living.

The cold form enclosed in "the narrow house" before us is alike insensible to our sorrows and our ceremonies. He has gone to accomplish the destiny of all our race, and his body to the profound slumber of the grave, there to be resolved with its original elements.

What, then, are all the externals of human dignity, the power of wealth, the dreams of ambition, the pride of intellect, or the charms of beauty, when Nature has paid her just debt!

The monarch at whose bidding nations pay obedience, and the poor beggar at his gate, are equals in the hour of death. The one must part with his sceptre and crown, the other has no further use for his wallet and rags; and each is indebted to Mother Earth for a common sepulchre. In the grave all ranks are leveled, and all distinctions are done away.

Our present meeting and proceedings will have been vain and useless if they fail to excite our serious reflections and strengthen our resolutions for amendment.

Let us each embrace the present moment, and while time and opportunity offer, prepare for that hour which must surely come, when the pleasures of this world will cease, and when the reflections consequent upon a well-spent life will alone afford us comfort and consolation.

Let us here resolve to maintain, with greater assiduity, the dignified character of our profession. May our faith be evinced in a correct moral walk and deportment; may our hope be bright as the glorious mysteries that will be revealed hereafter; and our charity boundless as the wants of humanity.

And, having faithfully discharged a portion of the great duties which we owe to God, to our neighbor, and ourselves, when at last it shall please the Grand Master of the Universe to send His Tiler, Death, to summon us into His eternal presence, may the record of our whole lives pass such inspection that it may be given unto each of us to "eat of the hidden manna," and to receive the "white stone with a new name written," that will insure perpetual and unspeakable happiness in the Paradise of God.

W. M. (or Chaplain). May we be true and faithful, and may we live and die in love.

Brethren. So mote it be.

W. M. (or Chaplain). May we profess what is good, and always act agreeably to our profession.

Brethren. So mote it be.

W. M. (or Chaplain). May the Lord bless us and prosper us, and may all our good intentions be crowned with success.

Brethren. So mote it be.

W. M. (or Chaplain). Glory be to God in the highest; on earth, peace! good will toward men!

Brethren. So mote it be now and forevermore. Amen.

The S. W. will now remove the apron (and other insignia if any) from the coffin, and hand it to the W. M.

An appropriate hymn will then be sung, during which the remains will be lowered into the grave. The Master then proceeds:

W. M. Forasmuch as it has pleased Almighty God, in His wise Providence, to take out of the world the spirit of our departed brother, we therefore commit his body to the ground. Earth to earth, ashes to ashes, dust to dust.

The Worshipful Master, holding up the apron, continues:

The lambskin, or white apron, is an emblem of innocence, and the badge of a Mason. It is more ancient than the Golden Fleece or Roman Eagle, more honorable than the Star and Garter.

The Worshipful Master then deposits the apron in the grave.

This emblem I now deposit in the grave of our departed brother. Here we are reminded of the universal dominion of death. The arm of friendship cannot interpose to prevent his coming;

the wealth of the world cannot purchase our release, nor will the innocence of youth or the charms of beauty propitiate his purpose.

The Worshipful Master, holding up the evergreen in his right hand continues:

This evergreen is an emblem of our faith in the immortality of the soul. By this we are reminded of our high and glorious destiny beyond the "world of shadows," and that there dwells within our tabernacle of clay an imperishable immortal spirit, over which the grave has no dominion and death no power.

We consign the body of our beloved brother to its kindred dust (drop sprig of evergreen).

We commend his spirit to God who gave it (raise right hand above head).

And cherish his memory here (place right hand over heart).*

*The Funeral Grand Honors may also be given.

The brethren will now move in procession around the grave, and severally drop into it the sprig of evergreen.

---

*Both arms are crossed on the breast, the left uppermost, the open palms of the hands striking the shoulders. They are then raised above the head, the palms of the hands striking each other—then dropped on the thighs, with the head bowed.

The funeral dirge (Pleyel's Hymn) may be sung. The Worshipful Master then continues the ceremony as follows:

From time immemorial it has been the custom among the Fraternity of Free and Accepted Masons, at the request of a brother, to accompany his remains to the place of interment, and there to deposit them with the usual formalities.

In conformity to this ancient usage, and at the request of our departed brother, we have assembled at this time, in the character of Masons, to offer the last tribute of our affection, and thereby demonstrate, in the strongest possible manner, the sincerity of our esteem for him, and our steady attachment to the principles of the fraternity.

Having with the usual Masonic ceremonies committed the body of our brother to its kindred dust, we leave him in the hands of a Being who doeth all things well.

To his immediate relatives and friends, who are most heart-stricken at the loss we have all sustained, we can most truly say that we deeply, sincerely and most affectionately sympathize with you in your afflictive bereavement, and would remind you that He who "tempers the wind to the shorn lamb" looks down with infinite compassion upon the widow and the fatherless in the hour of their desolation, and will fold the arms of His love and protection around those who put their trust in Him.

Then let us, brethren, so improve this warning that, when at last the record of our lives is finished, we may receive the thrilling invitation, "Come, ye blessed, inherit the kingdom prepared for you from the foundation of the world."

The following, from the California Burial Service, may be used in the discretion of the Worshipful Master:

Soft and safe to thee, my brother, be this, thine earthly bed; bright and glorious be thy rising from it. May the earliest buds of Spring unfold their beauties over this, thy resting place; and here may Summer's last rose linger longest. Though the cold blast of autumn may lay them in the dust, and for a time destroy the loveliness of their existence, yet their destruction is not final; for, in the gentle springtime, they will bloom again.

So, my brother, in the bright morning of the world's resurrection may this, thy body, now laid low by the chilling blast of death, come forth again in immortal glory, in realms beyond the sky. Until then, my brother, farewell, farewell!

Let us pray.

PRAYER.

Almighty and most merciful God, in whom we live, and move, and have our being, and before whom all men must appear to render an account for the deeds done in the body, we do most earnestly beseech Thee, as we now surround the grave of our departed brother, to impress upon our minds the solemnity of this day.

May we ever remember that "In the midst of life we are in death," mindful that life's opportunities pass swiftly, and, once gone, can never return; may we be diligent to improve them, and "apply our hearts unto wisdom."

And, O gracious Father, vouchsafe us, we pray Thee, Thy divine assistance, to redeem our misspent time; and in the discharge of the duties Thou hast assigned us in the erection of our moral edifice, may we have wisdom from on high to direct us, strength commensurate with our tasks to support us, and the beauty of holiness to render all our performances acceptable in Thy sight.

And at last, when our labors on earth are ended, may we obtain an entrance into that spiritual home, that house not made with hands, eternal in the Heavens.

Brethren. So mote it be.

The procession is then reformed and returns to the Lodge room, where the Lodge is closed in due form.

The following hymns may be used during the ceremony instead of Selections I. and II.

HYMNS THAT MAY BE USED.—L. M.

MUSIC—Hamburg.

Unveil thy bosom, faithful tomb,
  Take this new treasure to thy trust
And give these sacred relics room
  To slumber in the silent dust.

Nor pain, nor grief, nor anxious fear,
  Invade thy bounds; no mortal woes
Can reach the silent sleepers here,
  And angels watch their soft repose.

Break from His throne, Illustrious morn;
  Attend, Oh Earth, His sovereign word;
Restore thy trust; a glorious form
  Shall then ascend to meet his Lord.

SOFTLY NOW THE LIGHT OF DAY.

Softly now the light of day
　Fades upon our sight away.
Free from care, from labor free
　Lord we would commune with Thee.

Thou whose all pervading eye
　Naught escapes, without, within,
Pardon each infirmity
　Open fault and secret sin.

Soon from us the light of day
　Shall forever pass away.
Then from sin and sorrow free
　Take us, Lord, to dwell with Thee.

LODGE OF SORROW.

Preparation of the Hall.

The Lodge-room should be appropriately draped in black, and the several stations covered with the same emblem of mourning.

On the Master's pedestal is a skull and lighted taper.

In the center of the room is placed the catafalque, which consists of a rectangular platform, about six feet long by four wide, on which are two smaller platforms, so that three steps are represented. On the third one should be an elevation of convenient height, on which is placed an urn. The platform should be draped in black, and a canopy of black drapery may be raised over the urn.

At each corner of the platform will be placed a candlestick, bearing a lighted taper, and near it, facing the East, will be seated a brother, provided with an extinguisher, to be used at the proper time.

During the first part of the ceremonies the lights in the room should burn dimly.

Arrangements should be made to enable the light to be increased to brilliancy at the appropriate point of the ceremony.

On the catafalque will be laid a pair of white gloves, a lambskin apron, and, if the deceased brother had been an officer, the appropriate jewel of his office. Where the Lodge is held in memory of several brethren, shields bearing their names are placed around the catafalque.

OPENING THE LODGE.

The several officers being in their places, and the

brethren seated, the Master will call up the Lodge, and say:

W. M. Brother Senior Warden: For what purpose are we assembled?

S. W. To honor the memory of those brethren whom death hath taken from us; to contemplate our own approaching dissolution; and, by the remembrance of immortality, to raise our souls above the consideration of this transitory existence.

W. M. Brother Junior Warden: What sentiments should inspire the souls of Masons on occasions like the present?

J. W. Calm sorrow for the absence of our brethren who have gone before us; earnest solicitude for our own eternal welfare, and a firm faith and reliance upon the wisdom and goodness of the Great Architect of the Universe.

W. M. Brethren: Commending these sentiments to your earnest consideration, and invoking your assistance in the solemn ceremonies about to take place, I declare this Lodge of Sorrow opened.

The Chaplain or Master will then offer the following or some other suitable Prayer:

Great Architect of the Universe, in

whose holy sight centuries are but as days, to whose omniscience the past and the future are but as one eternal present, look down upon Thy children, who still wander amid the delusions of time—who still tremble with dread of dissolution, and shudder at the mysteries of the future; look down, we beseech Thee, from Thy glorious and eternal day into the dark night of our error and presumption, and suffer a ray of Thy divine light to penetrate into our hearts, that in them may awaken and bloom the certainty of life, reliance upon Thy promises, and assurance of a place at Thy right hand. Amen.

Response. So mote it be.

An appropriate Ode may here be sung.
The Master (taking the skull in his hand) will then say:

Brethren: In the midst of life we are in death, and the wisest cannot know what a day may bring forth. We live but to see those we love passing away into the silent land.

Behold this emblem of mortality, once the abode of a spirit like our own; beneath this mouldering canopy once shone the bright and busy eye; within this hollow cavern once played the ready, swift, and tuneful tongue; and now, sightless and mute, it is eloquent only in the lessons it teaches us.

Think of those brethren who, but a few days since, were among us in all the pride and power of life; bring to your minds the remembrance of their wisdom, their strength, and their beauty, and then reflect that "to this complexion have they come at last"; think of yourselves, thus will you be when the lamp of your brief existence has burned out. Think how soon death, for you, will be a reality. Man's life is like a flower, which blooms today and tomorrow is faded, cast aside, and trodden under foot.

When we look back upon the happy days of childhood, when the dawning intellect first began to exercise its powers of thought, it seems as but yesterday, and that, by a simple effort of the will, we could put aside our manhood, and seek again the loving caresses of a mother, or be happy in the possession of a bauble; and could we now realize the idea that our last hour had come, our whole earthly life would seem but as the space of time from yesterday until today.

Let these reflections convince us how vain are all the wranglings and bitterness engendered by the collisions of the world; how little in dignity above the puny wranglings of ants over a morsel of food or for the possession of a square inch of soil.

What shall survive us? Not, let us hope, the petty strifes and bickerings, the jealousies and heart-burnings, the small triumphs and mean advantages we have gained; but rather the noble thoughts, the words of truth, the works of mercy and justice, that ennoble and light up the existence of every honest man, however humble, and live for good when his body, like this remnant of mortality, is mouldering in its parent dust.

Let the proud and the vain consider how soon the gaps are filled that are made in society by those who die around them; and how soon time heals the wounds that death inflicts upon the loving heart; and from this let them learn humility, and that they are but drops in the great ocean of humanity.

<small>A suitable piece of music may now be sung.

At its conclusion, the Chaplain will read appropriate passages from Scripture.

An interval of profound silence will be observed. Twelve strokes will be slowly sounded on the bell. The lights in the Lodge room, if there be convenience, will be turned low, and the four brethren will extinguish the tapers near which they are placed. The Chaplain will then offer the following</small>

PRAYER.

Our Father Who art in Heaven, it hath pleased Thee to take from among us those who were our brethren. Let time, as it heals the wounds thus inflicted upon our hearts and on the hearts of those who were near and dear to them, not erase the salutary lessons engraved there; but let those lessons, always continuing distinct and legible, make us and them wiser and better. And whatever distress or trouble may hereafter come upon us, may we ever be consoled by the reflection that Thy wisdom and Thy love are equally infinite, and that our sorrows are not the visitations of Thy wrath, but the result of the great law of harmony by which everything is being conducted to a good and perfect issue in the fullness of Thy time. Let the loss of our brethren increase our affection for those who are yet spared to us, and make us more punctual in the performance of the duties that Friendship, Love, and Honor demand. When it comes to us also to die, may a firm and abiding trust in Thy mercy dispel the gloom and dread of dissolution. Be with us now, and sanctify the solemnities of this occasion to our hearts, that we may serve Thee in spirit and understanding. And to Thy name shall be ascribed the praise forever. Amen.

Response. So mote it be.

The Wardens, Deacons and Stewards will now approach the East and form a procession, thus:

Two Stewards, with rods.

Two Wardens, with Columns.

Deacon,   Deacon,
         The Master.
with rod.   with rod.

Which will move once around the catafalque to slow and solemn music.

On arriving in the East, the procession will halt

and open to the right and left. The Junior Warden will then advance to the catafalque and placing upon it a bunch of white flowers will say:

J. W. In memory of our departed brethren I deposit these white flowers, emblematical of that pure life to which they have been called, and reminding us that as these children of an hour will droop and fade away, so, too, we shall soon follow those who have gone before us, and inciting us so to fill the brief span of our existence that we may leave to our survivors a sweet savor of remembrance.

The Junior Warden will now return to his place, and an interval of profound silence will be observed.

The procession will again be formed, and move as before, to the sound of slow music, twice around the catafalque.

They will open as before, and the Senior Warden approaching the catafalque will place upon it a wreath of white flowers and say:

S. W. As the sun sets in the West, to close the day and herald the approach of night, so, one by one we lay us down in the darkness of the tomb to wait in its calm repose for the time when the Heavens shall pass away as a scroll, and man, standing in the presence of the Infinite, shall realize the true end of his pilgrimage here below. Let these flowers be to us the symbol of remembrance of all the virtues of our brethren who have preceded us to the silent land, the token of that fraternal alliance which binds us while on earth and which we hope will finally unite us in Heaven.

The Senior Warden returns to his place, and an interval of silence will be observed.

The procession will again be formed, and move three times around the catafalque to solemn music, as before.

Arrived in the East, the Master will advance and place upon the urn a wreath of evergreen, and say:

W. M. It is appointed unto all men once to die, and after death cometh the resurrection. The dust shall return to the earth and the spirit unto God who gave it. In the grave all men are equal; the good deeds, the lofty thoughts, the heroic sacrifices alone survive and bear fruit in the lives of those who strive to emulate them.

While, therefore, nature will have its way, and our tears will fall upon the graves of our brethren, let us be reminded by the evergreen symbol of our faith in immortal life that the dead are but sleeping, and be comforted by the reflection that their memories will not be forgotten; that they will still be loved by those who are soon to follow them; that in our archives their names are written, and that in our hearts there is still a place for them. And so, trusting in the infinite love and tender mercy of Him without whose knowledge not even a sparrow falls, let us prepare to meet them where there is no parting and where with them we shall enjoy eternal rest.

The Master will return to his place, and a period of silence will be observed.

The Chaplain will now be conducted to the altar, where he will read:

But some man will say: How are the dead raised up? and with what body do they come? Thou fool, that which thou sowest is not quickened except it die: and that which thou sowest, thou sowest not that body that shall be, but bare grain; it may chance of wheat or of some other grain: but God giveth it a body as it hath pleased Him, and to every seed his own body.

All flesh is not the same flesh; but

there is one kind of flesh of men, another flesh of beasts, another of fishes, and another of birds. There are also celestial bodies, and bodies terrestrial: but the glory of the celestial is one, and the glory of the terrestrial is another.

There is one glory of the sun, and another glory of the moon, and another glory of the stars; for one star differeth from another star in glory. So also is the resurrection of the dead. It is sown in corruption; it is raised in incorruption: it is sown in dishonor; it is raised in glory: it is sown in weakness; it is raised in power: it is sown a natural body; it is raised a spiritual body. There is a natural body and there is a spiritual body. And so it is written, The first man Adam was made a living soul; the last Adam was made a quickening spirit. Howbeit, that was not first which is spiritual, but that which is natural; and afterward that which is spiritual. The first man is of the earth, earthy: the second man is the Lord from Heaven. As is the earthy, such are they also that are earthy; and as is the heavenly, such are they also that are heavenly. And as we have borne the image of the earthy, we shall also bear the image of the heavenly.

Now this I say, brethren, that flesh and blood cannot inherit the kingdom of God; neither doth corruption inherit incorruption.

Behold, I shew you a mystery: We shall not all sleep, but we shall all be changed; in a moment, in the twinkling of an eye, at the last trump: for the trumpet shall sound, and the dead shall be raised incorruptible, and we shall be changed. For this corruptible must put on incorruption, and this mortal must put on immortality. So when this corruptible shall have put on incorruption, and this mortal shall have put on immortality, then shall be brought to pass the saying that is written, Death is swallowed up in victory. O death, where is thy sting? O grave, where is thy victory?

As the Chaplain pronounces the concluding words, "O grave where is thy victory?" the lights in the Hall will be raised to brilliancy, the four brethren seated around the catafalque will relight the tapers.

The Chaplain will return to his place in the East, and a suitable Ode of a cheerful character may be sung.

The Orator will then pronounce the Eulogium.

Another appropriate Ode may then be sung.

CLOSING.

W. M. Brother Senior Warden, our recollection of our departed friends has been refreshed, and we may now ask ourselves, Were they just and perfect Masons, worthy men, unwearied toilers in the vineyard, and possessed of so many virtues as to overcome their faults and shortcomings? Answer these questions, as Masons should answer.

S. W. Man judgeth not of man. He whose infinite and tender mercy passeth all comprehension, whose goodness endureth forever, has called our brethren hence. Let him judge.

In ancient Egypt no one could gain admittance to the sacred asylum of the tomb until he had passed under the most solemn judgment before a grave tribunal.

Princes and peasants came there to be judged, escorted only by their virtues and their vices. A public accuser recounted the history of their lives, and threw the penetrating light of truth on all their actions. If it were adjudged that the dead man had led an evil life, his memory was condemned in the presence of the nation, and his body was denied the honors of sepulture. But Masonry has no such tribunal to sit in judgment upon her dead; with her, the good that her sons have done lives after them, and the evil is buried with their bones. She does require, however, that whatever is said concerning them shall be the truth; and should it ever happen that a Mason dies of whom nothing good can be truthfully said, she will mournfully and pityingly bury him out of her sight in silence.

W. M. Brethren, let us profit by the admonitions of this solemn occasion, lay to heart the truths to which we have listened, and resolve so to walk that when we lay us down to the last sleep it may be the privilege of the brethren to strew white flowers upon our graves and keep our memories as a pleasant remembrance.

Brother Senior Warden, announce to the brethren that our labors are now concluded, and that it is my pleasure that this Lodge of Sorrow be closed.

S. W. Brother Junior Warden, the labors of this Lodge of Sorrow being ended, it is the pleasure of the W. M. that it be now closed. Make due announcement to the brethren, and invite them to assist.

J. W. Brethren, the labors of this Lodge of Sorrow being ended, it is the pleasure of the W. M. that it be now closed.

W. M. Let us unite with our Chaplain in an invocation to the Throne of Grace.

* * * * * *

W. M. This Lodge of Sorrow is now closed.

CONSECRATING AND CONSTITUTING NEW LODGES.

Preparation for Consecration of New Lodges.

The following preparations should be made before the Grand Lodge is convened, and the Worshipful Master of the new Lodge should attend to all details connected therewith.

A plain box about 4x8 inches should be neatly covered with bleached muslin and placed upon a stand or small table about equal distance between the Altar and the East.

The stand should be covered with a white table-cloth and the box placed thereon, and over all should be another white table-cloth reaching nearly to the floor.

The elements of consecration, Corn, Wine and Oil, are carried by the Deputy Grand Master (golden goblet), Grand Senior and Junior Wardens (silver goblets). These articles are provided by the Grand Lodge, and are to be found in the trunk containing the Grand Lodge aprons and other paraphernalia, which is forwarded by the Grand Secretary to the Worshipful Master of the new Lodge in advance of the ceremonies.

When all is ready for the Ceremonies of Consecration the three lesser lights should be placed in triangular form around the stand upon which rests the box representing the Lodge and the Grand Master informed that the new Lodge is ready to receive him.

On the day and hour appointed, the Grand Master (or the brother duly authorized by him to perform the service) and the officers, meet in a convenient

CONSECRATING NEW LODGES. 149

room near the Lodge to be constituted, and open in the Master Mason's Degree.

After the officers of the new Lodge are examined by the Deputy Grand Master, they send the following message to the Grand Master:

Most Worshipful Grand Master: The officers and brethren of ———— Lodge, who are now assembled in their Lodge-room, have instructed me to inform you that the Most Worshipful Grand Lodge was pleased to grant them a charter, authorizing them to form and open a Lodge of Free and Accepted Masons in the town of ————————. They are now desirous that their Lodge should be consecrated, and their officers installed in due and ancient form, for which purpose they are now met, and await the pleasure of the Most Worshipful Grand Master.

The Grand Lodge will then proceed to the hall of the new Lodge, and enter.

When the Grand Lodge enters, the Lodge is called up and a suitable hymn is sung while the officers and members of the Grand Lodge form parallel lines on each side of Altar, facing inward.

The brethren composing the Grand Lodge enter in single file, and are arranged in such manner that the Grand Stewards stand on opposite sides immediately in front of the emblematic Lodge, the Deputy

Grand Master on the right and Grand Senior and Junior Wardens on the left of the Grand Master.

When the Grand Lodge is in position, the Worshipful Master of the new Lodge introduces the Grand Lodge, and the Grand Honors are given.

The Deputy Grand Master then addresses the Grand Master as follows:

Most Worshipful Grand Master. A number of brethren, duly instructed in the mysteries of Masonry, having assembled together at stated periods by virtue of a dispensation granted them for that purpose, do now desire to be constituted into a regular Lodge, agreeably to the ancient usages and customs of the fraternity.

The Grand Master then says:

Right Worshipful Deputy Grand Master. The records, having been examined by a committee, were found to be correct, and were approved and the action of the committee affirmed by the Grand Lodge.

Upon due deliberation, the Grand Lodge have granted the brethren of the new Lodge a charter, establishing and confirming them in the rights and privileges of a regularly constituted Lodge, which the Grand Secretary will now read.

After the Charter is read, the Grand Master then says:

We shall now proceed, according to ancient usage, to constitute these brethren into a regular Lodge.

CONSECRATION.

The Grand Master and the Grand officers all devoutly kneel.

A piece of solemn music is performed while the Lodge is uncovered.

After which the first clause of the Consecration Prayer is rehearsed by the Grand Master or Grand Chaplain, which is as follows:

Great Architect of the Universe, Maker and Ruler of all worlds, deign from Thy celestial temple, from realms of light and glory, to bless us in all the purposes of our present assembly. We humbly invoke Thee to give us at this and at all times wisdom in all our doings, strength of mind in all our difficulties, and the beauty of harmony in all our communications. Permit us, Thou Author of light and life, great Source of love and happiness, to erect this Lodge, and now solemnly to consecrate it to the honor of Thy Glory.

Glory be to God on high. Amen.
Response by the brethren. As it was in the beginning, is now, and ever shall be, world without end. Amen.

So mote it be.

The brethren arise.

The Deputy Grand Master takes the golden vessel of Corn, and the Grand Senior and Junior Wardens take the silver vessels of Wine and Oil, and sprinkle the elements of consecration upon the Lodge.

The Grand Master or Grand Chaplain then continues:

Grant, O Lord, our God, that those who are now about to be invested with the government of this Lodge may be imbued with wisdom to instruct their brethren in all their duties. May Brotherly Love, Relief, and Truth always prevail among the members of this Lodge; and may this bond of union continue to strengthen the Lodges throughout the world.

Bless all our brethren, wherever dispersed, and grant speedy relief to all who are either oppressed or distressed.

We affectionately commend to Thee all the members of Thy whole family. May they increase in grace, in the knowledge of Thee, and in the love of each other.

Finally, may we finish all our work here below with Thy approbation, and then have our transition from this earthly abode to Thy heavenly temple above, there to enjoy light, glory, and bliss ineffable and eternal!

Glory be to God on high. Amen.

Response by the brethren. As it was in the beginning, is now, and ever shall be, world without end. Amen.

A piece of solemn music is rendered while the Lodge is covered.

The Grand Master or the Grand Chaplain then dedicates the Lodge in the following terms:

To the memory of the HOLY SAINTS JOHN we dedicate this Lodge. May every brother revere their character and imitate their virtues.

Glory be to God on high. Amen.

Response by the brethren. As it was in the beginning, is now, and ever shall be, world without end. Amen.

So mote it be.

A piece of music is rendered.

CONSTITUTION.

The Grand Master then constitutes the new Lodge in the form following, all the brethren standing.

In the name of the Most Worshipful Grand Lodge, I now constitute and form you, my beloved brethren, into a regular Lodge of Free and Accepted Masons. From henceforth I empower you to meet as a regular Lodge, constituted in conformity to the rites of the Craft and the charges of our ancient and honorable fraternity. And may the Supreme Architect of the Universe prosper, direct and counsel you in all your doings. Amen.

Response by the brethren. So mote it be.

INSTALLATION OF OFFICERS.

The Grand Master says:

The new Lodge having been solemnly consecrated and dedicated, we will now proceed to constitute this new Lodge by installing its officers.

The officers of the new Lodge then vacate their respective stations and places, and divest themselves of the jewels of office, which are given to the Grand Marshal and placed by him near the Altar.

The Grand Master then addresses the Grand Marshal:

Brother Grand Marshal, arrange the officers selected to conduct the affairs of this Lodge for the ensuing Masonic year in front of the Altar.

The officers are arranged before the Altar according to rank, the Worshipful Master on the right.

The Grand Master then says: Brother Grand Marshal, face the brethren to the West. Brethren, you now behold before the Altar the officers who have been selected to preside over the affairs of this Lodge. If any of you have any reasons to urge why they should not be installed, you will now make them known, or else forever hereafter hold your peace.

Hearing no objections, I shall proceed to install them.

The Grand Master then says:

Brother Grand Marshal, face the brethren to the East. Brethren, place your right hand over your heart, say I, pronounce your names, and repeat after me:

I, ———— ————, promise, upon the honor of a Mason, that I will, to the best of my ability, conform to and abide by the Ancient Landmarks, regulations and usages of Masonry, the Constitution and Edicts of the Grand Lodge, and faithfully perform the duties of the office to which I have been selected.

The officers are now all seated, except the Worshipful Master, who is introduced by the Grand Marshal in the following words:

Most Worshipful Grand Master, I present my worthy Brother ——— ———, to be installed Master of this new Lodge. I find him to be of good morals and great skill, true and trusty, and as he is a lover of our whole fraternity, wheresoever dispersed over the face of the earth, I doubt not that he will discharge his duties with fidelity.

The Grand Master then continues:

Brother, previous to your investiture, it is necessary that you should signify your assent to those ancient charges and regulations which point out the duty of the Master of a Lodge.

Continue as in Annual Installation Ceremony, as given on page 87 of this Manual, commencing with paragraph Numbered 1. Say "this new Lodge" in all cases where "this Lodge" occurs, concluding:

Finally, my brethren, as this fraternity

has been formed and perfected in so much unanimity and concord, in which we greatly rejoice, so may it long continue. May you long enjoy every satisfaction and delight which disinterested friendship can afford. May kindness and brotherly affection distinguish your conduct as men and as Masons. Within your peaceful walls may your children's children celebrate with joy and gratitude the transactions of this auspicious solemnity. And may the tenets of our profession be transmitted through your Lodge, pure and unimpaired, from generation to generation.

The Grand Marshal then makes the following proclamation.

In the name of the Most Worshipful Grand Lodge of the State of Wisconsin, I proclaim this new Lodge by the name of ——— Lodge No. —, duly constituted, and its officers installed.

I proclaim it in the South. I proclaim it in the West. I proclaim it in the East.

Brethren, together on the Grand Honors.

Addresses are then in order.

LAYING FOUNDATION STONES.

The laying of the corner or foundation stone of an edifice in accordance with Masonic Rites can be performed only by the Grand Lodge. The foundation stone thus laid, if it be for a Masonic building, is usually placed in the northeast corner. As the foundation upon which the entire structure is supposed to rest, it is considered by operative masons as the most important stone in the edifice. The symbolism of the stone when duly laid with Masonic Rites is full of significance which refers to its form, its situation, its permanence and to its consecration.

THE CEREMONY.

The time having been appointed, the Grand Lodge is convened in special communication and opened by the Grand Master, or by some Brother duly appointed for that purpose.

Everything being in readiness, the procession is formed in the following order:

Music.

Templars, or other organizations,
when provided to act as escort.

Master Masons.

(When a number of Lodges participate in the ceremonies, Lodges will be formed in the usual manner, and take their places in the procession in numerical order.)

THE GRAND LODGE,

under the direction of the Grand Marshal, will be formed in the following order:

Grand Tiler, with drawn Sword.
Grand Stewards, with white Rods.
Architect, with Square, Level and Plumb.
Grand Pursuivant and Grand Sword Bearer.
Grand Secretary and Grand Treasurer.
Grand Junior and Senior Wardens.
Master Mason carrying the Holy Writings.
Grand Chaplain.
Grand Junior and Senior Deacons.
Deputy Grand Master.
Grand Master.

Civil officers of the city or state when joining in the procession will be formed in the rear of the Grand Lodge.

Arriving at the site of the new building, the Grand Lodge will pass the escort and take their position upon the platform provided. The Grand Master will command silence, and the ceremony will begin with the singing of some suitable ode or anthem.

The Grand Chaplain offers a prayer.

The Grand Secretary, by order of the Grand Master, then reads a list of the various articles to be deposited in the stone.

The Grand Treasurer then deposits the box containing the several articles in the cavity prepared for that purpose.

The cornerstone, upon which is engraved the year of Masonry, the name of the Grand Master, and such other particulars as may be deemed necessary, is now lowered into its place. During the ceremony soft music is rendered by the band.

The principal Architect then presents the working tools to the Grand Master, who hands the Square to the Deputy Grand Master, the Level to the Grand Senior Warden, and the Plumb to the Grand Junior

Warden; when the Grand Master addresses the Grand Officers as follows:

Grand Master. R. W. Deputy Grand Master: What is the proper jewel of your office?

Deputy Grand Master. The Square.

Grand Master. What are its moral and Masonic uses?

Deputy Grand Master. To square our actions by the Square of Virtue, and prove our work.

Grand Master. Apply the implement of your office to that portion of the foundation stone that needs to be proved, and make report.

The Deputy applies the Square to the stone and says:

Deputy Grand Master. Most Worshipful Grand Master: I find the stone to be square. The Craftsmen have performed their duty.

Grand Master. R. W. Grand Senior Warden, what is the jewel of your office?

Grand Senior Warden. The Level.

Grand Master. What is its Masonic use?

Grand Senior Warden. Morally, it reminds us of equality, and its use is to lay horizontals.

Grand Master. Apply the implement of your office to the foundation stone, and make report:

This is done.

Grand Senior Warden. Most Worshipful Grand Master: I find the stone to be level. The Craftsmen have performed their duty.

Grand Master. R. W. Grand Junior Warden, what is the proper jewel of your office?

Grand Junior Warden. The Plumb.

Grand Master. What is its Masonic use?

Grand Junior Warden. Morally, it teaches rectitude of conduct, and we use it to try perpendiculars.

Grand Master. Apply the implement of your office to the several edges of the foundation stone, and make report.

This is complied with.

Grand Junior Warden. Most Worshipful Grand Master: I find the stone is plumb. The Craftsmen have performed their duty.

Grand Master. This cornerstone has been tested by the proper implements of Masonry. I find that the Craftsmen have skillfully and faithfully performed their duty, and I do declare the stone to be well formed, true and trusty, and correctly laid, according to the rules of our ancient Craft.

Let the elements of Consecration now be presented.

Corn.

The Deputy Grand Master comes forward with the vessel of Corn, and, scattering it on the stone, says:

I scatter this corn as an emblem of plenty. May the blessings of bounteous Heaven be showered upon us and upon all like patriotic and benevolent undertakings, and inspire the hearts of the people with virtue, wisdom and gratitude. Amen.

Response by the brethren. So mote it be.

Wine.

The Grand Senior Warden then comes forward

with the vessel of Wine, and pours it upon the stone, saying:

I pour this wine as an emblem of joy and gladness. May the Great Ruler of the Universe bless and prosper our National, State and City governments, preserve the union of the States, and may it be a bond of Friendship and Brotherly Love that shall endure through all time. Amen.

Response by the brethren. So mote it be.

Oil.

The Grand Junior Warden then comes forward with the vessel of Oil, which he pours upon the stone, saying:

I pour this oil as an emblem of peace. May its blessings abide with us continually, and may the Grand Master of Heaven and earth shelter and protect the widow and orphan, shield and defend them from the trials and vicissitudes of the world, and so bestow His mercy upon the bereaved, the afflicted and the sorrowing, that they may know sorrow and trouble no more. Amen.

Response by the brethren. So mote it be.

The Grand Master, standing in front of all, and extending his hands, makes the following

INVOCATION.

May the all-bounteous Author of Nature bless the inhabitants of this place with an abundance of the necessaries, conveniences, and comforts of life; assist in the erection and completion of this building; protect the workmen against every accident; long preserve the structure from decay, and grant to us all a supply of the Corn of nourishment, the Wine of refreshment, and the Oil of joy. Amen.

Response by the brethren. So mote it be.

The Grand Master strikes the stone three times with the gavel, and the Public Grand Honors* are given.

The Grand Master then delivers over to the Architect the implements of architecture, saying:

---

* The Public Grand Honors are given in the following manner: Both arms are crossed on the breast, the left uppermost, and the open palms of the hands sharply striking the shoulders; they are then raised above the head, the palms striking each other, and then made to fall smartly upon the thighs. This is repeated three times.

Worthy Sir (or Brother): Having thus, as Grand Master of Masons, laid the foundation stone of this structure, I now deliver these implements of your profession into your hands, intrusting you with the superintendence and direction of the work, having full confidence in your skill and capacity to conduct the same.

An appropriate anthem may be sung.

The Grand Master, or any other Master Mason, may then address the assembly.

DEDICATING MASONIC HALLS.

INSTRUCTIONS.

The brethren will assemble in the hall at the hour designated, clothed in white gloves and aprons and dark clothes. All entitled to do so will wear their jewels.

All present Masters of Lodges will take seats upon the left of the Master's station, and all Past Masters upon the right of the Master's station.

The Grand officers will assemble in some suitable room, where the Grand Lodge will be opened in form. After opening, the Grand Lodge will, if it appear in public, repair to the hall where the ceremony of dedication is to take place, in the following order:

Tiler, with drawn Sword.
Stewards, with White Rods.
Grand Secretaries.
Grand Treasurers.
A Past Master, bearing the Holy Writings, Square and Compasses.
Chaplain and Orator.
Past Grand Wardens.
Past Deputy Grand Masters.
Past Grand Masters.
Grand Junior Warden, carrying a silver vessel with Corn.
Grand Senior Warden, carrying a silver vessel with Wine.
Deputy Grand Master, carrying a golden vessel with Oil.
Grand Master,
Supported by two Deacons, with Rods.

Grand Standard Bearer.
Grand Sword Bearer, with drawn Sword.
Grand Pursuivant.

During the entrance of the Grand Lodge the following ode shall be sung, Brethren all standing.

TUNE—Italian Hymn.

Hail, universal Lord!
By Heaven and earth adored,
All hail, great God!
From Heav'n, Thy dwelling place,
Send down Thy saving grace,
Remember now our race,
O Lord our God!

Hail, universal Lord!
By Heaven and earth adored,
All hail, great God!
Before Thy Throne we bend,
To us Thy grace extend,
And to our prayer attend,
All hail, great God!

O, hear our prayer today,
Turn not Thy face away,
O Lord our God!
Heaven, Thy dwelling-place,
Can not contain Thy grace;
Remember now our race,
O Lord our God!

God of our fathers, hear,
And to our cry be near,
Jehovah, God!
The Heaven eternal bow,
Forgive in mercy now
Thy suppliants here, O Thou
Jehovah, God!

The Worshipful Master of the Lodge shall then address the Most Worshipful Grand Master as follows:

Most Worshipful Grand Master: The brethren of this Lodge, being animated by a desire to promote the honor and interests of the Craft, have prepared a Masonic hall for their convenience and accommodation. They are desirous that the same should be examined by the Most Worshipful Grand Lodge, and should it meet their approbation, that it be solemnly dedicated to Masonic purposes, agreeably to ancient form and usage.

The Architect or Brother who has had the management or supervision of the structure or Lodge hall, then addresses the Grand Master as follows:

Most Worshipful Grand Master: Having been intrusted with the superintendence and management of the workmen employed in the erection of this edifice, and having according to the best of my ability, accomplished the task assigned me, I now return my thanks for the honor of this appointment, and beg leave to surrender the implements which were committed to my care when the foundation of this fabric was laid (presenting to the Grand Master the Square, Level and Plumb), humbly hoping that the exertions which have been made on this occasion will be crowned with your approbation, and that of the Most Worshipful Grand Lodge.

To which the Grand Master makes the following reply:

Brother Architect: The skill and fidelity displayed in the execution of the trust reposed in you at the commencement of this undertaking, have secured the approbation of the Grand Lodge, and they sincerely pray that this edifice may continue a lasting monument of the taste, spirit and liberality of its founders.

An ode in honor of Masonry may here be sung.

The Deputy Grand Master then rises and says:

Most Worshipful Grand Master: The hall in which we are now assembled, and the plan upon which it has been constructed, having met with your approbation, it is the desire of the fraternity that it should now be dedicated according to ancient form and usage.

The Most Worshipful Grand Lodge having examined the several apartments, and the same having met with their approbation, they now desire that they should be dedicated to Masonic purposes agreeably to ancient form and usage.

Grand Master: Right Worshipful Brother, the Grand Lodge will comply with your wishes and now proceed to dedicate these apartments according to the forms and usages of Ancient Craft Masonry.

Brother Grand Stewards, you will uncover the Lodge.

A piece of music may now be rendered.

Right Worshipful Grand Chaplain, let us invoke the blessing of Deity.

Grand Chaplain: O Thou preserver of men! graciously enable us now to dedicate this house, which we have erected, to the honor and glory of Thy name, and mercifully be pleased to accept this service at our hands.

May all who shall be lawfully selected to rule herein, according to our Constitutions, be under Thy special guidance and protection, and faithfully observe and fulfill all their obligations to Thee and to the Lodge over which they may be called to preside.

May all who come within these consecrated walls have but one heart and one mind, to love, to honor, to fear and to obey Thee, as Thy majesty and unbounded goodness claim; and to love one another, as Thou hast loved us. May every discordant passion be here banished from our bosoms. May we here meet in Thy presence as a band of brethren, who, created by the same Almighty Parent, are daily sustained by the same beneficent hand, and are traveling the same road to the gates of death. May Thy Holy Word lie always before us in our Lodges, and virtue, love, harmony and peaceful joy reign triumphant in our hearts. Amen.

Response by the brethren. Glory be to God on high, on earth peace, good will toward men.

Instrumental music may be rendered while the Grand Officers are taking their places.

The Grand Lodge form in procession in the following order—one rank:

Marshal.
Grand Tiler.
Grand Senior and Junior Deacons.
Grand Treasurer and Secretary.
Grand Junior Warden, with Vessel of Corn.
Grand Senior Warden, with Vessel of Wine.
Deputy Grand Master, with Vessel of Oil.
Grand Master.

All the other brethren keep their places and assist in rendering the ode which continues during the procession, excepting only at intervals of dedication.

ODE—Music—Old Hundred.

Genius of Masonry, descend,
  And with thee bring thy spotless train:
Constant our sacred rites attend,
  While we adore thy peaceful reign.

The procession being around the Lodge, the Grand Master having reached the East, the Grand Junior Warden presents the vessel of Corn to the Grand Master, saying:

Most Worshipful Grand Master: In the dedication of Masonic Halls, it has been the custom from time immemorial to pour Corn upon the Lodge, as an emblem of Nourishment. I, therefore, present you this vessel of Corn, to be employed by you according to ancient usage.

The Grand Master, then striking thrice with his gavel, pours the Corn upon the Lodge, saying:

In the name of the great Jehovah, to

whom be all honor and glory, I do solemnly dedicate this hall to Freemasonry.

The Grand Honors are given once.

Bring with thee virtue, maid!
　Bring Love, bring Truth, bring Friendship here;
While kind relief shall lend her aid,
　To soothe the wrinkled brow of care.

After the second procession is made around the Lodge, the Grand Senior Warden presents the vessel of Wine to the Grand Master, saying:

Most Worshipful Grand Master: Wine, the emblem of Refreshment, having been used by our ancient brethren in the dedication and consecration of their Lodges, I present you with this vessel of Wine, to be used on the present occasion according to ancient Masonic form.

The Grand Master then sprinkles the Wine upon the Lodge, saying:

In the name of the Holy Saints John, I do solemnly dedicate this hall to Virtue.

The Grand Honors are twice repeated.

　　Bring Charity, with goodness crowned,
　　　Encircled in thy heavenly robe,
　　Diffuse thy blessings all around,
　　　To every corner of the globe.

After the third procession is made around the Lodge, the Deputy Grand Master presents the vessel of Oil to the Grand Master, saying:

Most Worshipful Grand Master: I present you, to be used according to ancient custom, this vessel of Oil, an emblem of that Joy which should animate every bosom on the completion of every important undertaking.

The Grand Master then sprinkles the Oil upon the Lodge, saying:

In the name of the whole fraternity, I do solemnly dedicate this hall to Universal Benevolence.

The Grand Honors are thrice repeated.

To Heaven's high Architect all praise,
All praise, all gratitude be given,
Who deigned the human soul to raise,
By mystic secrets, sprung from heaven.

The Grand Chaplain, standing before the Lodge, then makes the following

INVOCATION.

And may the Lord, the giver of every good and perfect gift, bless the brethren here assembled in all their lawful undertakings, and grant to each one of them, in need, full supply of the Corn of nourishment, the Wine of refreshment, and the Oil of joy. Amen.

Response. So mote it be.

Grand Master. Brother Stewards, you will cover the Lodge.

An appropriate address may be delivered at this time by the Grand Master or some brother appointed for that purpose, or the following may be used:

Brethren: The ceremonies we have performed are not unmeaning rites, nor the amusing pageants of an idle hour, but have a solemn and instructive import. Suffer me to point it out to you, and to impress upon your minds the ennobling sentiments they are so well adapted to convey.

This hall, designed and built by Wisdom, supported by Strength, and adorned in Beauty, we have consecrated in the name of the Great Jehovah; which teaches us, in all our work, begun and finished, to acknowledge, adore, and magnify Him. It reminds us, also, in His fear to enter the door of the Lodge, to put our trust in Him while passing its trials, and hope in Him for the reward of its labors.

Let then its altar be devoted to His service, and its lofty arch resound with His praise! May the eye which seeth in secret, witness here the sincere and unaffected piety which withdraws from the engagements of the world to silence and privacy, that it may be exercised with less interruption and less ostentation.

Our march around the Lodge reminds us of the travel of human life, in which Masonry is an enlightened, a safe, and a pleasant path. Its tesselated pavement of mosaic work intimates to us the checkered diversity and uncertainty of human affairs. Our step is time; our progression, eternity.

Following our ancient constitutions, with mystic rites we have dedicated this hall to the honor of Freemasonry.

Our best attachments are due to the Craft. In its prosperity we find our joy, and in paying it honor, we honor ourselves. But its worth transcends our encomiums, and its glory will outsound our praise.

Brethren, it is our pride that we have our names on the records of Freemasonry. May it be our high ambition that they should shed a lustre on the immortal page!

The hall is also dedicated to Virtue.

This worthy appropriation will always be duly regarded while the moral duties which our sublime lectures inculcate with affecting and impressive pertinency, are cherished in our hearts and illustrated in our lives.

Freemasonry aims to enliven the spirit of Philanthropy, and promote the cause of Charity, so we have dedicated this hall to Universal Benevolence, in the assurance that every brother will dedicate his affections and his abilities to the same generous purpose; that while he displays a warm and cordial affection for those who are of the fraternity, he will extend his benevolent regards and good wishes to the whole family of mankind.

Such, my brethren, is the significant meaning of the solemn rites we have just performed, because such are the peculiar duties of every Lodge. I need not enlarge upon them now, nor show how they diverge, as rays from a center, to enlighten, to improve and to cheer the whole circle of life. Their import and their application is familiar to you all. In their knowledge and their exercise, may you fulfill the high purposes of the Masonic institution.

How many pleasing considerations, my brethren, attend the present occasion! While in almost every other association of men, political animosities, contentions and wars interrupt the progress of Humanity and the cause of Benevolence, it is our distinguished privilege to dwell together in peace, and engage in plans to perfect individual and social happiness. While in many other nations our fraternity is viewed by politicians with suspicion, and by the ignorant with apprehension, in this country its members are too much respected, and its principles too well known, to make it the object of jealousy or mistrust. Our private assemblies are unmolested, and our public celebrations attract the general approbation of the fraternity. Indeed, its importance, its credit, and, we trust, its usefulness, are advancing to a height unknown in any former age. The present occasion gives fresh evidence of the increasing affection of its friends; and these apartments, fitted up in a style of such elegance and convenience, do honor to Freemasonry, as well as reflect the highest credit on the Lodge for whose accommodation and at whose expense it is erected.

We offer our best congratulations to the Worshipful Master, Wardens, officers and members of ——————— Lodge No. ———. We commend their zeal, and hope it will meet with the most ample recompense. May this hall be the happy resort of piety, virtue and benevolence. May it be protected from accident, and long remain a monument to the zeal and energy of the brethren of this Lodge, and an honor to Freemasonry. And when they, and we all, shall be removed from the labors of the earthly Lodge, may we be admitted to the brotherhood of the just, in the building of God, that house not made with hands, eternal in the heavens.

A piece of music may be rendered.

The Grand Lodge is again formed in procession as at first, returns to the room where it was opened, and is closed.

APRON ADDRESSES.

In cases where an actual gift is made of an apron, one of the following addresses may with propriety be used after the candidate has received the Master Mason's degree, and after the Charge:

* * * * * Lambskin, or White Leather Apron. It is an emblem of innocence and the badge of a Mason, more ancient than the Golden Fleece or Roman Eagle, more honorable than the Star and Garter, or any other order that could be conferred upon you, at this time or any future period, by king, prince, potentate, or any other person, except he be a Mason.

It may be that, in the coming years, upon your brow will rest the laurel leaves of victory; from your breast may yet hang jewels fit to grace the diadem of an Eastern potentate; nay, more than these, with light added to the coming light, your ambitious feet may tread round after round of the ladder that leads to fame in our mystic circle, and even the purple of our fraternity rest upon your honored shoulders; but never again from mortal hands—never again, until your enfranchised spirit shall have passed upward and inward through the pearly gates, shall any honor so distinguished, so emblematical of purity and of all perfection, be bestowed upon you, as this which I now confer. Let its pure and spotless surface be to you an ever-present reminder of an unblemished purity of life and rectitude of conduct; a never-ending argument for nobler deeds, for higher thoughts, for purer actions.

And when at last your weary feet shall have come to the end of their toilsome journey, and from your nerveless grasp shall drop forever the working tools of life, may the record of your life and conduct be as pure and spotless as this fair emblem which I now place in your hands. It is yours to wear throughout an honorable life, and at your death be placed upon the coffin which shall enclose your lifeless remains, and with them be laid beneath the clods of the valley.

And when at last your trembling soul stands naked. and alone before the Great White Throne may it be your portion, oh, my brother, to hear from Him who sitteth as the Judge Supreme the welcome words, "Well done, good and faithful servant. Enter thou into the joy of thy Lord."

By Past Grand Master C. C. Rogers.

"Masonry is a song of the human soul." Along its pathway, for centuries, courageous, manly men have trod the Master's carpet, drawing their inspiration from its sacred treasures of poetry, philosophy, tradition, art, science, history. Backward lies the past, upon whose milestones are inscribed the wisdom of our Masonic lore. About us, the transcendent thought and life of men, who today lend dignity and stability to our Craft, while before us lies the future, resplendent with the brightest hope.

At your initiation, and at the very threshold of this Lodge, you were taught that the lambskin was an emblem of innocence and the badge of a Mason.

The king, wrapped in his purple robes; the judge, clothed in his ermine; the statesman, crowned with the laurel wreath of fame, as well as he with sunburnt face, who earns his daily bread by the sweat of his brow, have each deemed it an honor to wear this emblem of innocence, this badge of a Mason.

To keep alive the memory of this occasion, the brethren of this Lodge have requested me to present you with such an apron. Now the sunlight of hope gladdens your heart, and the vigor of health and manhood is pictured upon your countenance, yet on the morrow your eyes may be closed in eternal sleep, and then this apron will be laid upon your coffin. But so long as life shall last, my brother, wear it so that no word of reproach will ever come to you, or the fraternity which has entrusted it to your keeping.

Accept it, then, with the blessing and benediction of the brethren who surround you.

Finally, when the fateful hour comes, on which you too must descend into the narrow house, into that better life, whose billows kiss the eternal shore, may it be in the words of the poet:

"Like one who wraps the drapery of his couch about him and lies down to pleasant dreams."

By Past Grand Master Eugene S. Elliott.

I now have the pleasure of presenting you with the lambskin or white apron. It is an emblem of innocence and the badge of a Mason, more ancient than the Golden Fleece or Roman Eagle, more honorable than the Star and Garter, when worthily worn. And from a time when the memory of man runneth not to the contrary, this emblem, plain and unadorned, has been the peculiar clothing of all Free and Accepted Masons. The Prince commanding the resources of empires and the citizen toiling in humble poverty, have alike worn it with the consciousness that it has lightened the labors of the one, and added dignity to the powers of the other. It may be that you are, or yet will be, so firmly intrenched in the hearts of your fellow men and so deserving of their gratitude, that they will elevate you to the highest positions of honor, trust and emolument, and cause your name to be inscribed high upon the pillars of worldly fame.

But never before have you had, and never again, my brother, will you have a higher mark of favor and confidence bestowed on you than this, which I, as the representative of these brethren, and of the Craft throughout the world, am about to bestow.

This emblem, worn by King Solomon when arrayed in all his glory, and which invested with additional dignity the immortal Washington, and which has been eagerly sought and worthily worn by the best men of your own generation, I now present to you. If you disgrace it, the disgrace will be augmented by the consciousness that within this Lodge you have been taught the principles of a correct and moral walk.

Its spotless white is emblematical of that purity of life and uprightness of personal manhood which, we hope and expect, will hereafter distinguish you in all your social and personal affairs. It is now yours to wear, so long as the vital spark of life shall animate your mortal frame, and when at last, whether in youth, manhood or age, your spirit having winged its flight to that house not made with hands, and when amid the tears and sorrows of surviving relatives and friends, and by the hands of sympathizing Brother Masons, your body shall be lowered to the confines of that narrow house appointed for all living, it will still be yours, yours to be placed with the evergreen upon the coffin which shall enclose your remains, and be buried with you.

And may you so wear this emblem of spotless

white, my brother, that no act of yours shall stain its purity or cast reflections upon an institution which has outlived the fortunes of kings and the mutations of empires.

May you so wear it and so live, my brother, that "when your summons comes to join that innumerable caravan which moves to the pale realms of shade, where each shall take his chamber in the silent halls of death, thou go not like the quarry slave at night, scourged to his dungeon, but soothed and sustained by that unfaltering trust, approach thy grave like one who wraps the drapery of his couch about him and lies down to pleasant dreams."

MASONIC CALENDAR.

The Masons in all parts of the world working in the York and French Rites, add 4,000 years to the Christian era, calling it ANNO LUCIS—*Year of Light;* abbreviated A∴ L∴; thus the year 1904 would be A∴ L∴ 5904.*

Masons practicing the ANCIENT ACCEPTED RITE use the Jewish Calendar, which adds 3,760 to the vulgar era, styled ANNO MUNDI—A∴ M∴—*Year of the World.* Or they sometimes use the Hebrew year, which begins on the 17th of September, or 1st of Tisri, using the initials A∴ H∴—ANNO HEBRAICO—*Hebrew Year.*

ROYAL ARCH MASONS date from the building of the second temple—530 years before Christ. Their style is therefore ANNO INVENTIONIS—A∴ INV∴—*in the Year of the Discovery.*

ROYAL AND SELECT MASTERS frequently use the common Masonic date—*Anno Lucis*—but properly they should date from the completion of Solomon's Temple, which would add 1,000 to the Christian era. Their style is ANNO DEPOSITIONIS—A∴ DEP∴—*in the Year of the Deposit.*

KNIGHTS TEMPLAR date from the organization of the Order—1118. Their style is therefore ANNO ORDINIS—A∴ O∴—*in the Year of the Order.*

---

*This fact has a symbolic reference, not because they believe Freemasonry is but that the principles and light of the institution are, coeval with the creation.

MASONS OF THE YORK RITE begin the year on the 1st of January; but in the FRENCH RITE it commences on the 1st of March.

BRO. A. G. MACKEY, in his *"Lexicon of Freemasonry,"* gives the subjoined rules for discovering the different dates:

1. *To find the date for the York Rite,* add 4,000 to the present year.

2. *To find the date for the Ancient Accepted Rite,* add 3,760 to the present year.

3. *To find the date for the Royal Arch,* add 530 to the present year.

4. *To find the date for the Royal and Select Masters,* add 1,000 to the present year.

5. *To find the date for the Knights Templar,* subtract 1,118 from the present year.

SAINTS JOHN DAYS.

Saint John the Baptist—June 24th.

Saint John the Evangelist—December 27th.

THE LEVEL AND THE SQUARE.

BY ROB. MORRIS, DD., LLD.

We meet upon the Level and we part upon the Square—
What words of precious meaning those words Masonic are!
Come, let us contemplate them; they are worthy of a thought—
With the highest and the lowest and the rarest they are fraught.

We meet upon the Level, though from every station come—
The king from out his palace and the poor man from his home;
For the one must leave his diadem without the Mason's door,
And the other finds his true respect upon the checkered floor.

We part upon the Square, for the world must have its due;
We mingle with its multitude, a cold, unfriendly crew;
But the influence of our gatherings in memory is green,
And we long, upon the Level, to renew the happy scene.

There's a world where all are equal—we are hurrying toward it fast—
We shall meet upon the Level there, when the gates of death are past;

We shall stand before the Orient, and our Master will be there,
To try the blocks we offer by His own unerring Square.

We shall meet upon the Level there, but never thence depart;
There's a mansion—'tis all ready for each zealous, faithful heart;
There's a mansion and a welcome, and a multitude is there,
Who have met upon the Level and been tried upon the Square.

Let us meet upon the Level, then, while laboring patient here—
Let us meet and let us labor, tho' the labor seem severe.
Already in the western sky the signs bid us prepare
To gather up our working tools and part upon the Square!

Hands round, ye faithful craftsmen, in the bright, fraternal chain;
We part upon the Square below, to meet in Heaven again.
Oh, what words of precious meaning those words Masonic are—
We meet upon the Level and we part upon the Square.

A MASONIC GEM.

The following gem was written by Brother Rob. Morris, and recited by him in the course of an address to the Grand Lodge of Wisconsin on his first visit to this State, in June, 1861.

Who wears the Square upon his breast,
Does in the eye of God attest,
   And in the face of man,
That all his actions will compare
With the divine, the unerring square,
   That squares great Virtue's plan;
  And he erects his edifice,
   By THIS design—and THIS—and THIS.

Who wears the Level, says that pride
Does not within his soul abide,
   Nor foolish vanity;
That man has but a common doom,
And from the cradle to the tomb,
   An equal destiny;
  And he erects his edifice,
   By THIS design—and THIS—and THIS.

Who wears the Plumb, behold how true
His words and walk! And could we view
   The chambers of his soul,
Each hidden thought, so pure and good,
By the stern line of rectitude
   Point up to Heaven's goal;
  And he erects his edifice,
   By THIS design—and THIS—and THIS.

Who wears the G, that mark divine,
Whose very sight should banish sin,
    Has faith in God alone;
His Father, Maker, Friend, he knows;
He vows and pays to God his vows
    Before the eternal throne;
  And he erects his edifice,
  By THIS design—and THIS—and THIS.

Thus life and beauty come to view,
In each design our fathers drew
    So glorious and sublime;
Each breathes an odor from the bloom
Of gardens bright beyond the tomb,
    Beyond the flight of time;
  And bids us build on THIS—and THIS,
  The walls of God's own edifice.